The Holy Spirit
in the World Today

THE HOLY SPIRIT
IN THE WORLD TODAY

EDITED BY JANE WILLIAMS

ISBN: 978 1 905887 91 0

Acknowledgments
Chapters 1, 6: Unless otherwise marked, scripture quotations are from The Revised Standard Version of the Bible copyright © 1346, 1952 and 1971 by the Division of Christian Education of the National Council of Churches in the USA. Used by permission. All rights reserved.
Chapters 2, 5: Unless otherwise marked, scripture quotations are taken from the Holy Bible New International Version. Copyright © 1973, 1978, 1984 by International Bible Society. Used by permission of Hodder & Stoughton Publishers, a member of the Hachette Livre UK Group. All rights reserved. "NIV" is a registered trademark of International Bible Society. UK trademark number 1448790. Chapters 7, 8: Scripture quotations marked [NIV] are also taken from The Holy Bible New International Version.
Chapters 3, 7, 8, 9 10, 11: Unless otherwise marked, scripture quotations are from The New Revised Standard Version of the Bible copyright © 1989 by the Division of Christian Education of the National Council of Churches in the USA. Used by permission. All Rights Reserved. Chapters 1, 4, 5: Scripture quotations marked [NRSV] are also taken from The New Revised Standard Version of the Bible.
Chapter 4: Unless otherwise marked, scripture quotations from the Good News Bible published by the Bible Societies and HarperCollins Publishers, © American Bible Society 1994, used with permission.
Chapter 4: Scripture quotation marked [NKJV] is taken from the New King James Version. Copyright © 1982 by Thomas Nelson, Inc. Used by permission. All right reserved.
Chapter 5: Scripture quotation marked [TNIV] is taken from the Holy Bible, Today's New International Version. Copyright © 2004 by International Bible Society. Used by permission of Hodder & Stoughton Publishers. A member of the Hachette Livre UK Group. All rights reserved. 'TNIV' is a registered trademark of International Bible Society.
p. 62: Extract from 'Flightline' by Micheal O'Siadhail from *Our Double Time*. Reproduced by permission of Bloodaxe Books.
p. 73: Prodigal Son image is a photograph of the original sculpture by Charlie Mackesy.

A catalogue record of this book is available from the British Library

Published by Alpha International
Holy Trinity Brompton
Brompton Road
London SW7 1JA
Email: publications@alpha.org

Contents

Contributors

Dr Luke Bretherton, Senior Lecturer in Theology and Politics at King's College London

Rt Revd Graham Cray, Archbishops' Missioner and Team Leader of Fresh Expressions

David F. Ford, Regius Professor of Divinity; Director, Cambridge Inter-Faith Programme, University of Cambridge

Tom Greggs, Professor of Historical and Doctrinal Theology, University of Aberdeen

Revd Dr Lincoln Harvey, Tutor in Theology at St Mellitus College

Jürgen Moltmann, Former Professor of Systematic Theology at the University of Tübingen

Dr Chris Tilling, Tutor in New Testament Studies, St Mellitus College

Revd Dr Graham Tomlin, Dean of St Mellitus College and Principal of St Paul's Theological Centre

Miroslav Volf, Professor of Systematic Theology at Yale University Divinity School

Dr Jane Williams, Tutor in Theology at St Mellitus College

Most Revd Dr Rowan Williams, Archbishop of Canterbury

Dr Simeon Zahl, Affiliated Lecturer in the Faculty of Divinity, University of Cambridge

FOREWORD

In May 2010, a quite remarkable conference took place. Each year, academic theological conferences take place where worthy and often eloquent papers are read, presenting ideas that can make you think in new ways and view theological questions differently. It often feels hard, however, to turn those to prayer, or to sense any attempt to engage with God in the midst of profound theological discussion. There are also numerous Christian conferences with heartfelt worship, practical motivational talks and fervent prayer, but which sometimes leave a sense of intellectual and existential dissatisfaction. The result is a common one – a sense that the life of the Christian mind, the life of the world, and the life of prayer, experience and worship do not belong together. It is a situation often lamented but not often rectified. This Holy Spirit in the World Today conference was an attempt to change this.

The conference involved the coming together of various streams. St Paul's Theological Centre (SPTC) began in 2005, as an attempt to do theology and theological training within one of the UK's most dynamic and innovative churches, Holy Trinity Brompton (HTB). This was the church that had seen the growth of the Alpha course from a local programme introducing people to the Christian faith into a global phenomenon, so that at the time of writing, over 6 million people across the world have taken the course that runs in around 50,000 churches worldwide, and in just about any denomination you can think of. It is also a church that, over the past twenty years, has seen a remarkable spiritual renewal, under the leadership of John Collins, Sandy Millar and now Nicky Gumbel – engaging with such diverse figures as John Wimber, Lesslie Newbigin and

Raniero Cantalamessa, Preacher to the Papal Household. In 2007, SPTC became part of St Mellitus College, a new theological institution launched by the Anglican Bishops of London (Richard Chartres) and Chelmsford (John Gladwin). The goal of the enterprise was to try to play its part in narrowing the gap between theology and the church, in the belief that the true home of theology is in the church, and that it will tend to become irrelevant and distorted if it loses that vital mooring.

St Mellitus, named after the very first bishop of London, is a distinct attempt to bring together different traditions of Christian expression, evangelical and Catholic, contemporary and traditional, in the belief that it is the Holy Spirit, rather than any particular doctrinal statement or liturgical practice, who brings true unity. Therefore it seemed appropriate, given the links to spiritual renewal in HTB, and the commitment to a fully rounded and generously orthodox Christian theology in St Mellitus, to explore the theology of the Spirit, but in a different way from normal academic conferences. As a result, we wanted to get the best possible theological reflection on pneumatology while doing this in the context of worship, prayer and the expectation of the presence and power of the Spirit.

The conference soon became known as the 'most significant theological conference of the year', its Twitter stream became the third highest trending theme in London over those two days, and for an academic conference, it drew a large number of delegates from professors to PhD students to pastors, reflecting this balance of the life of the church and engagement with serious theology. Professors Jürgen Moltmann from Tübingen, Miroslav Volf from Yale, David Ford from Cambridge, and Rowan Williams, the Archbishop of Canterbury, all spoke, alongside numerous others. There was worship led by the HTB worship band, meditative prayer based around Messiaen's 'Quartet for the End of Time', prayer ministry led by Sandy

Millar, ending with a time of prayer where theologians prayed for pastors, and pastors prayed for theologians, in a symbolic expression of the need for both and their interdependence on one another. This book is one of the outcomes of the conference, containing some of the key lectures given as part of the event. If the twenty-first century needs a theology *of* the Spirit, it also needs theology done *in* the Spirit. This conference was an attempt to do just that. As a mere book, it cannot convey the wider context of prayer and worship in which the talks were given. My hope would be that when read in a spirit of prayer, expecting the Spirit of God to touch its readers as they ponder these ideas, it may still achieve its purpose, of helping us think and pray in new ways in response to the Spirit who is at work in the church and the world, and who invites us into the knowledge of God and the future of his world.

Graham Tomlin

INTRODUCTION

In editing the contributions in this book, what struck me was what an unusual collection this is. It is not just the range of the contributors and the variety of styles, although that is in itself remarkable. It is the topic and the way it is tackled. We have become more accustomed, in recent years, to hearing about the Holy Spirit in theological debate and in Christian experience. Worshippers call upon the Holy Spirit and experience the Spirit's gifts; theologians discuss the Spirit in ways that have been really illuminating, particularly for the Christian understanding of the church. But this book reminds us that the Holy Spirit is not the possession of the faithful but the presence and action of the God who made the world. As always, Christians have been in danger of making God too small, and trying to confine God to our own interests and concerns. This book challenges us, instead, to see God at work, beyond our imagining, and allow ourselves to be drawn into that activity.

These essays had their origins in a two-day conference on The Holy Spirit in the World Today, the impetus for which came from a challenge: *is* the Holy Spirit to be found in the world? The answer has to be yes, otherwise we are saying that most of the life of the world is empty of God. That can be the perceived message of the church and of theology, but it cannot be the perceived message of Jesus. But the world is not just the beloved creation of God, it is also damaged and damaging; any discussion of the Holy Spirit in the world today needs not just to affirm but also to speak of challenge, of grief and of salvation. So contributors and participants came from many different Christian traditions, but all driven by the longing to honour the *fullness* of God's mission to the world that he loves.

The essays in this volume will give the reader, I hope, something of the flavour of the conference. All of us who took part found that our vision of God was too small. The conference did not comprise of just outstanding lectures, it also included Bible study, conversations, lectures, seminars. Even if just for a short time, we got a glimpse of what 'the church' might be – a place of hospitality for all who long to know Jesus, and are willing to be sent to the world, in the power of the Holy Spirit. This book is just the beginning of the conversation. We hope that readers will be drawn into it, and will come and participate in future conferences on this vital topic – and even run their own. Above all, we hope that more and more people will go in the power of the Spirit, and find the Spirit there ahead of them.

Jane Williams
St Mellitus College

1 THE CHURCH IN THE POWER OF THE SPIRIT

• JÜRGEN MOLTMANN

THE GATHERED COMMUNITY IS THE CRITICISM OF THE CHURCH AND ITS FUTURE

'Think globally – act locally!' That is what we learned in the ecumenical movement. And this is even more applicable for an understanding of the church. What you can't do locally in the place where you happen to be, you shouldn't expect globally of the church either. So I shall not begin with the global heaven of the Holy Spirit, but locally, on this earth, with my own congregation in Tübingen, the Jacobuskirche in the old city. I have noticed when giving lectures all over the world – from Korea to Nicaragua – that the more concrete you are, the more universally what you say will be understood. The universal is always concrete, so it is in the concrete that we have to discover what is universal.

Until 1919, the Protestant churches in Germany were state churches. Afterwards they called themselves *Volkskirchen* – churches for the people. But the structure remained and does so still. It is the *parochial system*. It is quite simple. When we moved to Tübingen, we lived in the Hausserstrasse, so we belonged to the Martinskirche. When we then moved to the Biesingerstrasse, we belonged to the Stiftskirche. The pastors were supposed to look after the religious and pastoral needs of their districts. That is what the church is for – looking after people; one 'belongs' to it, but seldom 'goes'. People in general are aware of its existence when there are baptisms, confirmations, weddings or funerals. If one goes to church, one is said to 'visit' the service. If one goes to Holy Communion, one counts as a Communion 'guest'. Of course there are kindergartens, youth groups, women's and men's groups, and social work. But the basic idea is that the people living in the district should be looked after, religiously speaking.

In Protestant Germany, this church for looking after people is organised in *Landeskirchen* – regional churches. This division dates back to the sixteenth century and at that time was based on the principle *cuius regio, eius religio* – your ruler's religion is yours too: one regional prince; one regional religion; one regional university; one theological faculty. If you look at a map showing the regional Protestant churches in Germany today, you can detect without any difficulty the little German states that still existed in the nineteenth century. Today, we in Tübingen are politically united in the *Land*, or province, of Baden-Württemberg, but as churches we are divided into Württemberg and Baden.

The first breakthrough in this regional-parochial system came about during the Nazi dictatorship when, with the help of the state party, the pro-Nazi, so-called German Christians (*Deutsche Christen*) took over many of the regional churches and installed German-Christian bishops. Resistance against this 'bringing into line' took form in the congregations of the Confessing Church. I use the word 'congregations' deliberately, because the Confessing Church was organised in voluntary congregations. They paid their pastors and curates themselves, and organised

15

themselves presbyterially in 'councils of brethren': there were councils of brethren in the congregations; in the regional churches; and in the church on a national level (the *Reichsbruderrat*). That was the church's democratic alternative to the authoritarian Führer principle of the Nazi dictatorship. For the first time in its 400-year-long history, Protestant Christianity in Germany gave itself its own constitution, a constitution independent of the state and in resistance against Nazi rule. This, following the Barmen Theological Declaration,[1] was the achievement of the synod in Berlin-Dahlem in the autumn of 1934.

Through their very existence, these independent and resisting congregations of the Confessing Church were a criticism of the established and conforming church. They were the thorn in the flesh of the church that had accommodated itself to the political conditions, and they were the promise of the future for the Church of Jesus Christ in Germany. The struggle between the German national religion dominated by the Nazis, and the congregations that confessed Christ was in concrete terms local and yet it had a universal significance for the whole of Christendom on earth.

That brings me to the present, and to my Jacobus congregation in Tübingen. At about the same time as I myself came to Tübingen, Pastor Karlfried Schaller arrived, and was given the ancient Jacobuskirche in the old city. He found that his Sunday congregation consisted of only about twenty old inhabitants belonging to his district. But then his congregational council took a decision. This said: 'The aim of all our efforts should be that, through the medium of an inviting congregation, as many people as possible should arrive at a personal relationship to Jesus as the Christ.'

---

1   The declaration approved by representatives of the Confessing Church in opposition to the pro-Nazi so-called German Christians. The declaration was mainly the work of Karl Barth.

This vision was given practical form through the following maxims:

1. The general expertise of all believers
2. What can't be done simply, simply can't be done
3. What doesn't happen regularly, generally hardly happens
4. The person who proposes the first step must take the second one too

With this model and these general rules, the congregation's growth began. From being a parochial congregation it turned into an attractive missionary congregation. Today one must arrive well before the start of the service if one wants to find a seat in the church – and that is unique, even in Tübingen. The inner secret of this congregation is community, fellowship. There are more than twenty house groups with different aims, and these groups present themselves regularly in the church services. A church for looking after people has turned into a participating congregation. But the orientation point was not the congregation's requirements but its gifts: 'We ask about people's preferences and strengths.' One has to start from what one is and can do, not from what one is not, and what one can't do.

Sunday worship is the focus for the congregation, and all the house groups are involved in the preparation. The artistically gifted decorate, bands offer new styles of music, Taizé chants are mixed with gospels, meditation on the sermon texts precedes the sermon. The Eucharist is accompanied by the humming of the congregation. A missionary, diaconal service for children, the sick and the old developed out of the church's worship. The 'Tübingen Table' for the hungry and homeless started with this congregation. The members form the congregation themselves, following their own faith. About 30 per cent of the congregation's members are Catholic, but that does not prevent the whole congregation from sharing together in the Lord's Supper.

Of course, the impulse for all this came first from a charismatic pastor who radiated a quite natural spirituality, but the congregation is independent. What doesn't happen through its members doesn't happen at all. Last year the pastor had to leave because he had reached retirement age. The congregation lived without a pastor for a whole year, and its services were just as thronged with people as before. It is a congregation with a number of 'lay preachers', as these mature Christians are wrongly called.

We are living in the exciting era in which the Constantinian form of the church is slowly coming to an end and something new is being pioneered. This new form is coming from below – from men and women who are saying: 'We are the church.'

THE CHARISMATIC CONGREGATION

I shall now leave the local world of Tübingen and come to something more global. We shall turn from the description of a specific congregation in the twenty-first century to the fundamental changes in today's world, and shall then ask 'What does the Spirit say to the churches?' By the 'charismatic congregation' of the heading, I mean what Paul describes in 1 Corinthians 12–14, and not yet what is today called 'the charismatic movement' or 'the Pentecostal churches'.

First, with the whole of Christendom on earth, we today confess our Christian faith. That was not always so. The great event of the twentieth century was *the end of the Christian nations* and *the rebirth of the church* in independent congregations with a universal mission and a universal hope for God's future for the world.

In the 'primal European catastrophe' of the First World War of 1914–18, the Christian nations destroyed each other mutually, after they had divided up the rest of the world into their colonies. In this war 'the Christian world' fell apart. 'Christian civilisation' foundered. 'The Christian era' came to an end. 'Holy Russia' became communist and atheist, the 'Holy Fatherland' of the Germans turned into the murderous Nazi dictatorship, and after a little delay it became possible to talk in England today about the 'Death of Christian Britain'.[2]

Whereas in the nineteenth century the churches had dissolved themselves into the Christianity of these separate states, after the catastrophe they experienced their resurrection and rebirth out of the ruins of Christendom. The church is no longer responsible for the religion of the state and the social unity of the state's society; it has to be mindful of its own prophetic form of existence. The Christian national religions disappeared. Denominationally mixed – and today multi-religious – societies developed in an age of so-called 'secularisation', which would probably be better described as the age of the individualisation of modern men and women.

It is a remarkable phenomenon that at the very same time, the ecumenical movement emerged, creating from national and minority churches the congregation of a worldwide Christian community. What each church represents in its society is not just that society's civil religion of its society; nor does it stand only for itself – it represents 'the whole of Christendom on earth'. In all the different and particular societies, the independent and ecumenical church represents universal forces and global tasks in the conciliar process that works for 'justice, peace and the preservation of creation'. To

---

2   Callum G. Brown, *The Death of Christian Britain* (London: Routledge, 2001).

put it simply, God has set us on our own feet, and he has set our feet in a broad place (Psalm 31:8).

Before the First World War, the 'Christian world', as it looked to the future, saw a world of progress, while in respect of the space of the earth it was a world of imperial colonisation, civilisation and mission. Modern times – which in German is called 'the new time' (*Neuzeit*) – were seen as the fulfilment of the dream of a Thousand Years' Empire. That was secularised millenarianism – the end of history. Today, out of the ruins of this shattered dream, a church is emerging that again hopes for the kingdom of God. This is a Christianity that in the terrors of our present time is again learning the long forgotten and suppressed cry: '*Maranatha*, come Lord Jesus, come soon.' That is the church of hope in the world's 'valley of the shadow'; that is the messianic people of God, who remain true to the suffering earth, because they expect the 'new earth in which righteousness dwells' (2 Peter 3:13). This church is about more than religion; it is about the new life. This church is about more than the church; it is about the kingdom of God. This church is about more than men and women; it is about the reconciliation of the cosmos.

Second, there is enough for everyone. The more a congregation stops being a church for looking after people's religious needs and turns instead into a living, participatory congregation, the more it will also become a partnership for the whole of life. Believers don't just come together for Sunday worship but are there for one another during the week too. Acts 4:32–35 describes the model:

> ... the company of those who believed were of one heart and soul ...
> they had everything in common ...
> There was not a needy person among them ...

This last sentence has always impressed me deeply: in the congregations of the risen Christ there is always 'enough for everyone'; there are no needy people. With their faith in Christ, they live in the presence of the Christ who has risen, and that means that they have been freed from the fear of death, and with that from the greed for life. They can live tranquilly and modestly. This is not a question about a communist social programme run by the first Christians; it is about their experience of fellowship in the Spirit of the risen Christ.

Is that a utopia? No, the monastic communities have always lived in this way. In the Reformation period the communities of brethren grew up: the Moravian brethren; the Mennonite settlements; the Hutterites; and the Amish. These Christian communities could be interpreted as a retreat from 'the wicked world', but also as radical alternatives to it. The Moravian community broke through the class society of the eighteenth century. Counts and peasant farmers, men and women, were brothers and sisters. During the socialist dictatorship, the Christian congregations counted as places of truth where one was not afraid to speak.

Today we are living in competitive societies of social advancement and decline, of winners and losers, with growing inequality and vanishing social cohesion. In this social situation congregations filled with the Spirit will become communities of mutual help and places of trust. People find here that in place of the fear evoked by competition they are met with respect and liking, in friendship and love. Here all are equal, wealth and poverty, ability and disability no longer define a person's value. Here all are respected in their human dignity as God's beloved image. Economic solidarity is only one outcome of this community lived in the presence of the risen Christ. The opposite of poverty is not wealth: the opposite of both poverty and wealth is community, for in community we shall be rich,

rich in friends, in brothers and sisters. In community we can generally help ourselves. In the Pentecostal experience we discover our riches in solidarity.

In the Pentecostal community the ancient promise given in the book of Joel becomes true:

And it shall come to pass afterward, that I will pour out my spirit on all flesh; your sons and your daughters shall prophesy, your old men shall dream dreams, and your young men shall see visions. Even upon the menservants and maidservants in those days I will pour out my spirit.

Joel 2:28–29

Young people who do not yet play a role in public life and older people who no longer fully participate in it will be the first to experience the spring of life that comes upon all flesh; a new equality between the generations emerges. Sons and daughters will prophesy. Men and women are equal in the community of the Spirit. There are no longer any male privileges. Menservants and maidservants receive the Spirit, and a new community of masters and servants comes into being. The Holy Spirit is no respecter of social distinctions. She puts an end to any class society. The Holy Spirit will always awaken these democratic and revolutionary energies until humanity becomes 'one heart and one soul'.

Third, we turn to the reconciled cosmos. The apostolate took Paul to the cities of the ancient world. His message about Christ brought people reconciliation with God. What God? We cannot discover from the letters written by the apostle and his followers, or from the other earliest Christian testimonies, that there was any 'interfaith dialogue' with the many cults and mysteries in the ancient cities, apart from the discussions with Judaism. Why not? I think it was because the apostolic gospel proclaimed not only the reconciliation of men and women but also the reconciliation of the cosmos with the God who made heaven and earth. It was not the other religions that interested the first Christians in the cities of the ancient world; what interested them was the de-demonisation and reconciliation of the cosmic forces and powers. According to Colossians 1:20, through Christ God has reconciled 'all things, whether on earth or in heaven'; according to Ephesians 1:10, Christ brings peace into the cosmos by uniting 'all things in him, things in heaven and things on earth'. The exalted Christ brings reconciliation and peace into the world of nature's chaotic forces. The Christian belief in creation frees human beings from the fear of nature and the deification of nature, and makes a life at peace with nature and in harmony with the cosmos possible.

That is as up to date today as it was then. How should we affirm and love a life visited by earthquakes, tsunamis and climate catastrophes unless we believe that Christ is Lord over the powers? It certainly makes a difference whether people are delivered over to incalculable natural forces or whether the earth rots away into the rubbish heap made by incalculable human beings. But it is the same gospel of cosmic peace through Christ's giving of himself for the reconciliation of the world.

Today's interfaith dialogue ministers to peace between the religions and to coexistence between the religious communities. That is valuable. But what is much more important, in my view, is the dialogue with the secular world about the politics of peace, social justice and the healing of the wounds which we have inflicted, and are still inflicting, on the organism of the earth. The missionary church will join with human rights groups, with the Social Forum, with Attac and with Greenpeace when the real issue is not religion but the cosmos. The reconciled cosmos belongs within the community of human beings reconciled with God in Christ. The church of Christ is a church of the new earth

23

too (2 Peter 3:13). In God's future this suffering earth has a tremendous future: it will become God's dwelling place and remain so eternally.

THE THIRD PARADIGM OF THE CHURCH

I believe that the new age of the church will be an age of the Holy Spirit. We are discovering 'the church in the power of God's Spirit' not because of any obscure apocalyptic prophecies but because of experiences in congregations in the present day.

What paradigms has the church known during its history?

1. The hierarchical paradigm
The church's first paradigm in the Byzantine–Roman world was 'the holy rule'. The 'monarchical episcopacy' was the known pattern from Ignatius of Antioch onwards: one God, one bishop, one church.

Politically, the one ruler on earth corresponds to the one God in heaven; religiously, the one high priest on earth, the *pontifex maximus*, corresponds to the one God in heaven. In its Christian form, the patriarch or the pope, *il Papa* in Rome, corresponds to God the Father. This unilinear structure is carried through by way of the bishops down to the priests. The hierarchical order consists of the clergy, the 'spirituals', who come to earth through God's Spirit. Subordinate to them are the people in the church, 'the laity'. The priest, *in persona Christi,* stands above the congregation, which through him receives the church's gifts of grace. A visible sign is the distribution of the Eucharistic Communion. The cup for the laity was hotly disputed. Another visible sign is male celibacy, and the exclusion of women from the priestly ministry. On the one hand, Vatican I put forward the idea about the pope's universal episcopacy. On the other, Vatican II recognised the general 'priesthood of all believers'.

24

In order to link the two, today the Roman Catholic Church talks about the *communio hierarchica*.

2. *The Christocentric paradigm*

Whereas the hierarchical paradigm took its legitimation from the monarchy of God the Father, the churches of the Reformation proceeded from Christ as the head of the church. The incarnate Son of God establishes the unity of his church. In what way? In that the only begotten Son of God is at the same time the firstborn among many brothers and sisters (Romans 8:29). His open, inviting brotherhood brings the many into fellowship with God and with each other. 'The Church is the congregation of the brethren [and sisters] in which Jesus Christ acts presently as the Lord in Word and sacrament through the Holy Spirit,' says the Barmen Theological Declaration of 1934 in Thesis III. The community of Christ makes the church a brotherly and sisterly community of equals. All are children of God through faith, all are equally priests and kings. The general 'priesthood of all believers' dissolves the division between priests and laity; there is no 'laity'; all Christians are 'spirituals' endowed with the Spirit.

According to the Reformation view, there is no division between theologians and laity either: all Christians who believe and understand are theologians. The church presents itself not through the hierarchy but through the synods of the congregations. The unity which is represented by a hierarchy is replaced by the covenant, on Israel's model, in the presbyterial-synodal order.

3. *The charismatic paradigm*

Many congregations today are experiencing the charismatic presence of the Holy Spirit. I mean this in Paul's sense, the way he describes it in 1 Corinthians 12–14. In a congregation that avails itself of its many gifts and energies, everyone is accepted as he or she is; everyone with their individual gifts and powers plays a part in the building up of the community and the spread of God's kingdom. No one has a higher or lower position as a result of what he or she can contribute to the congregation. 'When you come together, each one has a hymn, a lesson, a revelation, a tongue, or an interpretation. Let all things be done for building up', says Paul in 1 Corinthians 14:26 [NRSV]. 'There are varieties of gifts, but the same Spirit' (1 Corinthians 12:4). So there can't be any fear of pluralism, relativism or chaos, but simply trust in the one and uniting divine Spirit. The life-giving Spirit is the wellspring of the multiplicity of original powers and forms of life, which are as protean as creation. The Spirit gives everyone what is hers or his. Every member of the charismatic congregation is not merely a hearer of the word, and not only a child of God, but also an expert in his or her life and personal vital energies. Through the experiences of the Holy Spirit, the all-equalising brotherhood of Christ fans out into a multicoloured diversity of charismata. They are all 'full of the Holy Spirit', as is said of the first Pentecostal congregation. In the charismatic congregation Christians come of age, and acquire the courage to live out their own experience of faith and to bring themselves with their own powers into the community of the coming kingdom of God.

4. The eschatological renewal of the church
In the course of its history Christianity has experienced the hierarchical church of God the Father and the brotherly church of God the Son, and is now experiencing the charismatic church of God the Holy Spirit; and yet in the present day these forms of the church exist simultaneously and together and influence each other mutually. Cardinal Ratzinger observed a 'congregationalisation' of the Roman Catholic Church, and

in the Protestant churches all over the world today we are experiencing a kind of Pentecostalisation of the congregations. In the nineteenth century people talked about a sequence in salvation history – the church of Peter, the church of Paul, and the church of John. If we leave aside the belief in progress that went along with that, 'the church in the power of the Spirit' reminds us of the apocalyptic context of the Joel promise: there will be signs in the heavens and on the earth, blood, fire and columns of smoke, the sun will be turned to darkness ... (Joel 2:30–31). However it may be today in relation to 'the Last Days', the perils for human beings, life and the earth are growing, and we find the divine response which we can hope for echoed in Friedrich Hölderlin's words:

Where there is danger
deliverance also grows.

THE TRINITARIAN UNITY OF THE CHURCH

'Act locally – think globally!' That brings me back to the local Jacobus congregation in Tübingen, and makes me think at the same time about the wide heaven of the triune God.

First, some people think that the Christian doctrine of the Trinity is a vast mystery that not even theologians can understand. They consider it to be a speculation that has no significance for practical life. None of this is true. Simple life in the community of Christ has a threefold structure: I live in fellowship with Christ. His God and Father becomes my God and Father too. With him I cry 'Abba, dear Father!' In fellowship with Christ on the other hand I experience that his grace is 'new every morning'. I experience the living energies of God's Spirit; they comfort me and make me a living person. I don't just *believe* in the triune God; I *live* in the fellowship of Jesus, and of the

27

Father, and of the Holy Spirit. That is the open secret of the triunity. 'The grace of the Lord Jesus Christ and the love of God [the Father], and the fellowship of the Holy Spirit' is with us all (2 Corinthians 13:14).

Second, the church is founded and made alive neither solely through the monarchy of the Father, nor solely through the brotherhood of the Son, nor solely through the fellowship of the Holy Spirit, but through the joint efficacy and the unity of the Father and the Son and the Holy Spirit. Cyprian was right: 'The Church is the people united through the unity of the Father and the Son and the Holy Spirit.'

Jesus' prayer as we find it in John 17:21 also makes this clear:

> ... that they may all be one;
> even as thou, Father, art in me,
> and I in thee,
> that they also may be in us, so that the world may believe...

The community of believers corresponds to – 'even as' – the mutual indwelling of the Son in the Father and of the Father in the Son. Our fellowship is the reflection and impression of the Trinitarian fellowship of God. But it is more even than that: 'That they also may be in us.' The fellowship of believers lives mystically in the triune God. The triune God is the broad place in which we embrace each other, it is the field of force of the love which makes us, together with each other, living people; it is the open future which invites us to hope.

2 One Spirit, Many Tongues: Globalisation, Christian Faith and Religious Diversity[1]

MIROSLAV VOLF

I currently teach a course at Yale University on Faith and Globalisation, together with the former UK prime minister, Tony Blair. We have already taught this course three times, and we'll continue to do so in the future. For me, it has been an immensely rewarding and interesting engagement; I have enjoyed both our agreements and our disagreements and have learned a tremendous amount. Some of what follows is based on the discussions that we have had during that course. Indeed, that is how I will begin as I discuss the relationship between the Holy Spirit and the political realities of our lives, and tie this discussion to the issue of globalisation and religious diversity.

The assumption of the Faith and Globalisation course is that religious faith traditions and globalisation are among the most

---

1 This chapter is a transcript of a talk, and retains some features of the spoken word. I am grateful to Connie Gundry Tappy, who, with a deft editorial hand, has transformed the talk into the text. The talk itself was based on chapter 12 of my book *Allah: A Christian Response* (New York: HarperOne, 2011).

powerful forces shaping our world today. The future of the world will largely depend on how these two forces – which are partly colliding but also partly reinforcing one another – continue to relate. And one of the key questions that we are asking in that course is: How can we reconcile the conflict between faiths that results in part because the processes of globalisation are intertwining our world and pushing people closer together, while at the same time these processes are very rapidly changing the character of the world we inhabit and therefore leaving many people disoriented? The other side of the question is: How do we think about giving the processes of globalisation a more human face? In my judgement that question concerns not just the processes of globalisation themselves, but above all the very ends, the goals that we seek to achieve in both our individual and public lives. And that question of how to give a human face to globalisation turns out to be the more difficult one. Archbishop Williams addresses this issue in his chapter, and I think the great religious traditions – certainly the Christian faith – hold it as a central issue.

The very first session of our course was held on 11 September 2008, seven years after the attack on the Twin Towers and the Pentagon. The session was titled 'The Ambivalence of Faith', and it examined how faiths in fact function as an immense source for good, while at the same time being a source of destruction. So, after initial comments both by Mr Blair and by me, a Muslim graduate student, Yasir Qadhi, was the first to raise his hand. He made the following comments and then asked the following question:

Certain elements of faith are by definition exclusivist,
whether we would like them to be so or not; for example,
large segments of Christianity believe very strongly that
unless you accept Jesus Christ as your personal Lord and

Saviour, you're basically excluded from grace. That very belief is of course anathema to Muslims, so the question arises since we are not able to change these fundamental beliefs, how can we make people genuinely love and care about one another when they believe that that person who is outside their faith tradition is outside of God's grace?

That's the literal transcription of Qadhi's question. Now, he singled out Christians, but Muslims display the same exclusivity. Other religious groups do as well. One way to read his question would be to say that he is talking about interpersonal relationships – the ability of us as private persons to care for neighbours whom we consider to be somehow 'outside that grace', whether or not that's the right phrase.

But Qadhi's question was actually about politics. He was enquiring about the ability of people who belong to exclusivist faiths to advocate equal treatment of all people in the given state. How can we be expected to treat someone with whom we believe God is displeased in the same way as someone with whom we believe or know that God is pleased? Now, the idea of a secular and religiously neutral state is precisely that: equal treatment of all – of those with whom God is pleased and those with whom God isn't so pleased. Does loyalty to God then clash with loyalty to the state? If so, then religious exclusivism leads straight to political intolerance.

What was interesting to me was not so much that this question was raised, but that this question stayed with us throughout the whole course, from the very first session. In one way or another, most aspects of the intersection of faith and globalisation touch upon this question. Can religious exclusivists of differing religions live comfortably with one another under the same political roof? What kinds of political arrangements would we have to have for this to be possible? This question is most acute in the case of monotheists since monotheism is deemed to be the most intolerant of all creeds. It is this question that I want to pursue here. Towards the end I will then bring in the question of the Spirit and the Spirit's inspiring people to speak in many tongues and to pursue justice and generosity.

THE TRUE GOD AGAINST THE FALSE GODS

First, let's look at monotheism. Is monotheism by its very nature religiously and politically exclusivist? A well-known Egyptologist, Jan Assmann from the University of Heidelberg, has written extensively on the emergence of monotheism and has argued that monotheism is characterised not so much by belief in one God, but by the claim that the one God is the *true* God. The famous pre-Socratic Greek philosopher who influenced Plato and, with him, the whole of Western thought – Parmenides – distinguished strictly between truth and falsehood in the realm of knowledge. Jan Assmann suggests that Moses did the same in the realm of religion. Moses was the Parmenides of religion: he was the first to make a distinction between truth and falsehood in religion. Truth is opposed to falsehood; therefore, the true God is opposed to all false gods and idols, as well as opposed to all false conceptions of God, namely to all heresies. Now that's religious exclusivism!

But there is more. As it turns out, monotheism was not just a religious idea – it was often understood as a political project as well. One influential version of this political project goes something like this: the indivisible power of the single earthly ruler should mirror the indivisible power of the one God, and since the power of the one God extends through the whole of creation, so also should – in the ideal case – the power of the earthly ruler extend throughout the whole realm and throughout all the earth. Belief in the one true God, therefore, makes the centralised power of a single ruler to be imperialistic. Monotheism is not just religiously exclusivist; it is also politically imperialistic. Now religious exclusivism is underwriting aggressive political exclusivism.

If such aggressive exclusivism is in the DNA of the monotheism of devout Jews, Muslims and Christians, how then can they live peacefully together in a single world? How then can they peacefully pursue the common good? Of course, the defenders of monotheism would immediately respond by saying, 'No, no – monotheism is no worse in this regard than polytheism.' For polytheistic societies of the ancient world were not particularly known for their peacefulness, and when they went to war, they always took their gods with them. If one jumps through the centuries to the present time, the argument is that today Hinduism in India, for instance, doesn't seem to be more tolerant than Islam or Christianity is. Now let's assume that that response is correct, as I think it is. Even so, it does not take us as far as we need to go. It's kind of a victory in a small skirmish, but it's not a victory in a major, decisive battle. We need monotheism to be socially beneficial, not just as bad as polytheism! The latter is small comfort because it represents a concession to monotheism being aggressively exclusivistic.

That's where the response number two comes in: monotheism is democratising, the defenders of monotheism say. It's true, they concede, that monotheism has sometimes been used to support centralised forms of government. But take a look at the emergence of monotheism and you will see that it is a form of resistance to powerful, centralised forms of government. Recall when the Israelites decided they would really like to have a king. What happened? Judges upon whom the Spirit of the Lord fell to address particular issues that arose in society ruled over Israel. But then the Israelites decided that wasn't quite what they wanted. They wanted a king. The response of the Lord, the God of Israel was: '"I brought Israel up out of Egypt, and I delivered you from the power of Egypt and all the kingdoms that oppressed you." But you have now rejected your God, who saves you out of all your calamities and distresses. And you have said, "No, set a king over us"' (1 Samuel 10:18–19). So there is a *disjunction* between single, centralised rule of the earthly king and the one God. To have centralised rule embodied in a king is to reject God. Again, this is a good argument as far as it goes, but the bottom-up democratic forms of government can be quite intolerant. As a peek at any schoolyard will tell you, forms of exclusivism that emerge from the bottom up can actually be extraordinarily oppressive. So we need to affirm not just democratic strands of belief in one God, but also its compatibility with and its fostering of political pluralism.

Response number three tries to capture that idea and says: 'Monotheism is in fact inclusive, rather than being exclusive. Because God is one, the world God created is one as well – it's not divided in hostile regions of light and darkness, not split between competing powers, not divided between clashing moral visions. A single, unifying truth binds human beings, and the same demands of justice apply to all.' Agreed again, in part. But the trouble is that monotheism is universal and inclusive on its own terms. If you follow the one true God, then you're 'in'; if you don't follow the one true God, then you're 'out', so that exclusivism is sort of the obverse of monotheism's inclusivism. A decisive question, therefore, regarding the relationship between allegiance to one God and the ability of children of Abraham to coexist peacefully in a single state or a single world and pursue the common good is this: can they be religious exclusivists while embracing pluralism as a political project? In my judgement, that is really the central question we are facing.

Religious exclusivism — political pluralism

I don't think I have to explain too much about what religious exclusivism means. Different people will define it in slightly different ways, but I am using the term to describe the belief that one's own faith is a true way to God (or the true way of life, in case of non-theistic religions). 'Exclusivism' does not mean that all other faiths are completely false, but it does mean that one's own faith is true and is the best way to come to God, and that the truth of other faiths is measured by one's own beliefs. Thus religious exclusivism is opposed to religious pluralism, which says, basically, that different religious traditions are roughly equally true and roughly equally efficient as ways to scale the same mountain on the way to God.

We need to distinguish religious pluralism from political pluralism, or pluralism as a political project. By this latter I mean the following: for a state to count as politically pluralistic, two conditions must be satisfied. One condition is that the state does not favour one religion over others or one overarching interpretation of life over others; rather, the state is impartial towards them all. The second condition is that all folks from a variety of religious (and irreligious) perspectives can bring into the public domain their own visions of good life; no matter what their religious belief is, they have equal voice as anyone else does. This is an ideal type description of political pluralism: no state embodies it completely, and a state can count as politically pluralistic even if it embodies it partially. Its basic thrust is that the state ought to be impartial to all overarching perspectives of life, and that religious people ought to be able to bring their visions of good life into the public debate.

The key question is this: With these definitions of religious exclusivism and political pluralism, can one be a religious exclusivist and political pluralist at the same time? My response is an unambiguous 'yes', because I can point you to many people of this sort. For instance, the religious right in the United States are often charged with being among the nastier folk on the American political scene, but it can be easily shown that along with their religious exclusivism they're also political pluralists – for the most part they want to grant to others the same rights they have. Similar examples can be found in the Muslim world, particularly in Indonesia, where the Nahdatul Ulama is just one good example of such a group.

MONOTHEISM AND POLITICAL PLURALISM

And now for the crucial question: Can monotheist religious exclusivists be not just political pluralists, but political pluralists while being consistent with their basic religious convictions? Again, my answer is 'yes'. Here is the reason why. One of the important legacies of monotheism is considered to be the fact that the belief in one true God *gave religion an essential ethical dimension*. Earlier I noted that monotheism introduced to the world of religions the distinction between truth and falsehood. Related to it is another distinction, which is as important and as revolutionary as the distinction between truth and falsehood: the distinction between justice and injustice.

At the heart of monotheistic faiths is a concern for doing justice. Polytheistic religions, in whose environment monotheism arose, were primarily cultic religions, without a pronounced moral dimension; monotheism was fundamentally a moral religion. From the introduction of monotheism on, serving God meant doing good, doing justice. Of course, monotheism does not reduce religion to moral behaviour, but rather expands, so to speak, religion to include the pursuit of justice, the loving of our neighbour, all of which is essential to what it means to serve God. Indeed, ritual observance without moral rectitude is worse than empty – it is kind of a counterfeit religious coin often serving to make up for the absence of true piety, which is aligning one's character with God's and living so aligned in the world. The falsely pious person seeks divine approval for what manifestly is not worthy of divine approval. It is not that ritual is inherently falsely pious; rather, that ritual devoid of true piety is empty because it lacks, and often serves to mask a lack of, a necessary, moral dimension.

The one God to whom Christians exclusively owe allegiance commands love of one's neighbour, treating others in ways you yourself want to be treated, and presumably not treating others in ways you yourself do not want to be treated. This principle of reciprocity applies both to doing what is good and not doing what is wrong. And since one God is the God of all people, the principle of reciprocity applies to all people. Acting in accordance with this principle is, in part, what it means to worship God. Loving others is a genuinely religious act.

In addition to giving religion an essential ethical dimension, monotheism decoupled religion from the state and from ethnic belonging. From the start, monotheism's decoupling of religion from the *state* was arguably connected with the liberation of the children of Israel from slavery in Egypt. It involved a founding of an alternative form of social life in which human beings do not rule over other human beings; rather, they come together in freedom to place themselves under the rule of the covenant made with the one God, the one true Lord of all people. The ruler of the state does not rule in God's place; nevertheless, salvation is not identical with political rule – it is a gift of community from God.

In addition to this decoupling of religion from the state, a decoupling of religion from ethnic belonging also occurred. In Israel, the one God of all people remained attached in a special way to the Jewish people, the physical descendants of Abraham

37

and Sarah. The apostle Paul, the great missionary to the Gentiles, severed that link. He sensed in it an unresolved tension between the universality of the one God and the particularity of a single chosen people. And he insisted that all human beings, Jews and Gentiles, are included in the people of God on equal terms, on account of God's utterly gratuitous love rather than by virtue of any natural characteristic or achievement of their own.

That's where Pentecost comes in. The church, of course, was born on the day of Pentecost, and when the church was born the Holy Spirit fell on the apostles, who were assembled together; and those around them heard them speak in other tongues. Now, I am the son of a Pentecostal minister, and most of the speaking in tongues that I have heard has not been speaking in any recognisable language that I could tell. But the tongues speaking at Pentecost was different; it consisted of recognisable languages, which is to say that from the beginning the church has spoken in the languages of different peoples. Pentecost shows that the church was, from its beginning, multilingual, multicultural, multi-ethnic. This is of immense political significance.

What happens when the gospel is preached to all nations, in accordance with the belief that God is revealed in Jesus Christ as the God of all peoples and the God for all peoples? What happens when these different peoples speak the language of faith in their own language? The answer: churches will emerge, but they will emerge as new and foreign social bodies in their native nations. Every time the church emerges, it emerges as a foreign body in its particular social and cultural space.

My former colleague at Yale, Nicholas Wolterstorff, who is a leading Christian philosopher working on political theology and philosophy today, notes this crucial feature of the Christian church when he writes:

*On the one hand, its [the church's] membership included
people from other nations; on the other hand, its
membership never included all from any nation. The church
included more than Slavs and not all Slavs; the church is not
Slavic. The church includes more than Americans and not
all Americans; the church is not American. And so forth, for
all nations, all peoples. The church is not the church of any
nation or people. It does not belong to the social identity of
any people.*[2]

The church – a body of people giving ultimate allegiance to one
God as revealed in Jesus Christ – introduces a fissure within
the citizenry of a state. This fissure is a religious one, but as a
religious fissure it changes the very character of the state. As
Wolterstorff notes, the state can no longer 'express the shared
religious identity of the people, since there is no such identity'.
Wolterstorff continues:

*The coming of the church undermines the political vision
of the ancient Greek philosophers, that government is the
highest institutional expression of the religio-ethical bonds
uniting its citizenry. Wherever the church enters a society, it
destroys whatever religio-ethical unity that society may have
possessed. Now there is only religious pluralism.*[3]

THE COMING OF THE SPIRIT AND POLITICAL
PLURALISM

The decoupling of religion from the state and from ethnic
belonging – the second feature of monotheism that I highlighted

---

2 Nicholas Wolterstorff, *The Mighty and the Almighty* (unpublished manuscript), XI,
p. 4.
3 *Ibid.*

previously – is intimately tied to the character of the church as a community of the Spirit, a community that speaks many languages. The first feature of Christian monotheism that I mentioned earlier – doing of justice, loving one's neighbour understood as a religious duty, a form of worship of God – is also related to the coming of the Spirit.

I noted that the church began with the falling of the Spirit on the disciples gathered at Pentecost. But before the Spirit had fallen onto the disciples gathered in the Upper Room after Christ's ascension, the Spirit came upon Jesus Christ himself at the very beginning of his ministry. In his inaugural sermon, Jesus said: 'The Spirit of the Lord is upon me.' Significantly, the purpose of the Spirit's coming is not just so that Jesus would proclaim the good news for the soul, but so that he would enact it as well by doing of justice and enacting concretely love of all people, especially those who are sick and oppressed. The Spirit comes so that justice and love may reign among the people. If you take these two features of the Spirit of God together – the Spirit of justice and the Spirit of many cultures (as evidenced in the many languages spoken at the birth of the church) – what is the consequence for the relation between Christian faith and the state?

If my argument in the first part of this chapter was cogent, the presence of the Spirit furnishes us with excellent reasons to affirm pluralism as a political project. Since religion is not identical with the state but is a 'sub-culture' in each state, and since doing justice and loving our neighbours is a religious duty, we must affirm the appropriateness of religious pluralism within a given state and therefore the state's impartiality towards all religions as well as the right of each religious group to pursue its own religious vision of good life. For it would be patently unjust for the state to grant one religious community freedom to live according to the dictates of its god, while denying the corresponding freedom to others.

Because the Spirit does what in the New Testament the Spirit is said to do (1) states should be impartial to all religions, and (2) all religious communities should be allowed to live according to their own vision of good life and, if they wish, contribute to the shaping of the public debate as to how life ought to be lived in society as a whole. In my view, a consistent Christian religious exclusivist ought to be a political pluralist, and I believe that that view is the consequence of the coming of the Spirit at the very beginning of the Christian story – first the coming of the Spirit upon Jesus and second the coming of the Spirit on the day of Pentecost.

In conclusion, let me return briefly to the question of globalisation. Today one of the central questions we are facing in the context of globalisation is: How can we find resources (1) to be unabashedly who we religiously are, affirm our religious convictions as true, and at the same time (2) be able in a just and generous way to live in a world marked by diversity, to pursue the common good? That's a great challenge for us today. I believe the Christian faith gives us extraordinary resources to achieve exactly that goal, and as we go deeper into the life of the Spirit I hope that we will be not only more personally attuned to the character of Jesus Christ as the self-revelation of the one true God, but also and because of that attuning, be more able to live together in justice and peace with others in our complex world.

3 IN THE SPIRIT: LEARNING WISDOM, GIVING SIGNS

DAVID F. FORD

In this chapter I want to plunge straight into one big question about the Holy Spirit – that is, the definiteness with which Jesus can be identified, contrasted with the vagueness of the Holy Spirit. All Christians agree that one important thing to say about the Spirit is that it is the Spirit of Jesus Christ. The most vivid picture of this is in John 20, where the resurrected Jesus breathes the Holy Spirit on his disciples, sharing his own life breath – his Spirit – with them. Jesus can be identified fairly clearly – through what he said and did, and what happened to him in Palestine in the first century.

But think of his Spirit being shared with dozens, hundreds, thousands and even millions of others. Each is different, in various situations, relationships, cultures, speaking different languages, wearing different clothes, and so on. They do not simply repeat what Jesus said and did. Part of what the Spirit does is to inspire words and actions in new situations, shape different lives and communities. The Spirit generates glorious, endless particularity and diversity, shines in 10,000 different faces, speaks in 10 million distinctive voices. So how can the

Spirit be identified? All sorts of words, actions and sufferings claim to be in line with Jesus, in his Spirit. But it can be hard and confusing to try to identify the Spirit.

The language used to describe the Spirit warns us that it will not be easy to grasp. It is hard to grasp fire, wind, breath, water, light, power. Each of these is dynamic, mobile, hard to contain, abundant, generative. But just as there are sciences that try to do justice to fire and gases, to wind and weather, light and power, so theology has to tackle the challenge of thinking about the elusive Spirit. It requires many approaches, and this book is a good example of the range that is needed. What results is neither neat boxes or packages, nor clear concepts that wrap up the Spirit, but a stretching of our thinking, imagining and action to try to do justice to this most astonishing reality of all. As Christians today, we need above all to seek wisdom in the Spirit so that we can risk living in the Spirit in our particular situations and relationships, giving fresh signs of God's presence in the Spirit in the church and in the world.

I want first to reflect a little on the amazing reality of being in the Spirit; then ask what wisdom might be learned about living in the Spirit in the world today, and finally try to identify signs of the Spirit in today's world.

IN THE SPIRIT: IN GOD'S SPIRIT;
IN A FAMILY; IN A GLOBAL DRAMA

So what does it mean to be in the Spirit? The New Testament overwhelms us with language related in various ways to being in the Spirit – language to do with baptism, grace, being in Christ or in God, born from above, eternal life, fellowship, glory, blessing, gentleness, gifts, being transformed, having power and energy, being confident, speaking freely under pressure, enduring suffering, rejoicing in the Lord, and so on.

As we move through Christian history there are innumerable other ways of imagining, conceiving and embodying life in the Spirit, in the arts and literature, theology, liturgy, and above all in the lives of particular people and communities.

There is no one definitive way of patterning all this, and the Christian tradition has wisely let a thousand flowers bloom. But we do need to love God with all our minds in relation to the Spirit too, and therefore try to order our thinking appropriately while recognising that the reality will always overflow our concepts. So I am going to risk proposing three fundamental ways in which being 'in the Spirit' can be conceived.

1. In God's circumambient Spirit

The first is the most mysterious and pervasive, best expressed in the metaphors of air and wind. God is freely present as our ultimate environment, all-encompassing yet at the same time within us, both utterly public and radically intimate. In the story of Jesus and Nicodemus, John's Gospel interweaves the thoughts and images of seeing and entering the kingdom of God, being born from above (or born again), God's Spirit as wind blowing freely where it chooses, Jesus being lifted up on the cross, God loving the whole world, and eternal life (which, from this point on, becomes John's equivalent of the kingdom of God in the other Gospels). All of this would take many essays to explore, but for now the vital thing is the Spirit freely embracing us in God – like wind: in God's love; in God's realm and sphere; in God's eternal life.

A helpful concept for this has been suggested by David Kelsey in his recent 1,000-page work, *Eccentric Existence: A Theological Anthropology.*[1] It is, I think, the best new theological book that I have read in the past decade or more

---

1 Louisville: Westminster John Knox Press, 2009.

(I recommend it to any young theologian as a model for what thorough, profound and generously orthodox Christian thinking for the twenty-first century might be like – not all easy going, but so worthwhile!), and it includes a rich yet rigorous doctrine of the Holy Spirit.

In this book, David Kelsey proposes the term 'circumambient Spirit' (chapter 12A). The distinctive way God relates to us as the Holy Spirit is not primarily through being our Creator, or being among us in person as Jesus Christ, but through relating in a circumambient way. In this relationship, the Spirit draws us into God's future for us and for the whole of creation. The Spirit is always already there as our divine environment in which we live and breathe and move, and is also more intimate to us than we are to ourselves. We need not be caught divisively in the splits between public and private, inner and outer, body and mind, individual and social, present and future, ultimate and penultimate.

To live in the circumambient Spirit is to find those polarities coming together in living now future in prayer and worship something of the reality of God's, in Christian community and in hopeful engagement with God's world. The combination of publicity and intimacy is especially important, and vividly described in the two New Testament stories of the giving of the Spirit: in Acts 2 it is tempestuous and goes public in a dramatic form; in John 20 it is intimate, behind closed doors, face to face. The Spirit at the same time draws us deeper into loving God and each other and deeper into the world and its public life, and it embraces both movements circumambiently.

2. In the shared Spirit of God's family

The second way focuses, within life in the Spirit, on the fact that the Spirit is shared with others. This is what Paul calls the *koinonia*, or sharing, or communion, or fellowship of the Holy Spirit. His amazing letter, 2 Corinthians – on which I once spent five years writing a book with my colleague Frances Young, and at the end of it we both felt as if we had hardly begun to sound its depths – ends with this blessing: 'The grace of the Lord Jesus Christ, the love of God, and the *koinonia* of the Holy Spirit be with all of you' (2 Corinthians 13:13). Earlier in the letter we get a glimpse of the reality this involves.

*Now the Lord is the Spirit, and where the Spirit of the Lord is, there is freedom. And all of us, with unveiled faces, seeing the glory of the Lord as though reflected in a mirror, are being transformed into the same image from one degree of glory to another [*apo doxes eis doxan*]; for this comes from the Lord, the Spirit.*

2 Corinthians 3:17–18

Sharing in the Spirit means that together, in community, we are part of a dynamic set of relationships, each particular as each face is particular, involved with God and other people at the same time, and being transformed continually, from glory to glory, in unimaginably good ways.

This shared Spirit means, in a fundamental New Testament image, being part of a new family life. Paul, in Romans 8, one of his greatest passages on the Spirit, says:

For all who are led by the Spirit of God are children of God. For you did not receive a spirit of slavery to fall back into fear, but you have received a spirit of adoption. When we cry 'Abba! Father!' it is that very Spirit bearing witness with our spirit that we are children of God, and if children, then heirs of God and joint heirs with Christ – if, in fact, we suffer with him so that we may also be glorified with him.

Romans 8:14–17

The Spirit is the bonding of family life, and our continual crying out for the Spirit opens us up to relationships, conversations, commitments, collaborations – and sufferings – that are unimaginable in advance of entering into them; but when we are in them we realise that we are privileged to taste a little the experience of being transformed from glory to glory. The Spirit transforms the boundaries of our self, connects us to all those with whom God is connected for flourishing and blessing, and so we find ourselves part of a new family.

3. In God's global drama

The third way to think of being in the Spirit is as part of the ongoing drama of God bringing all of creation and history to its fulfilment. In theological terminology, it is about the eschatological Spirit, who draws us into God's future and gives tastes and signs of it now. John R. Levison, in his fine study, *Filled with the Spirit*, speaks of the Holy Spirit tying believers to the drama of God's promises.[2]

So much of our lives are shaped by trusting in promises and commitments, whether explicit or implicit. Marriage is one of the most obvious – with whom you live, where you live, your decisions about time and money, the long-term commitment to children, and much else are shaped by the strange reality of a promise. But so also is a great deal in business and financial life, in law, in friendship, in any group or community – and in baptism's covenant relationship with God, our promises responding to and embraced in God's promises. The Holy Spirit is central to these promises of God. The Spirit is seen as the first fruits of what is to come, as a down payment from God, guaranteeing the future that God promises, and as a seal on those promises. To live in faith is to trust and hope in God's

---

2   John R. Levison, *Filled with the Spirit* (Grand Rapids, MI: Eerdmans, 2009), p. 259.

promises, which are expressed in many ways: the kingdom of God, peace and justice for all, eternal life, glory, meeting God face to face in love, communion with God and with other people, worship in heaven, and so on. To live in the Spirit is to be called to play an active part in the drama through which God realises his promises.

LEARNING WISDOM IN THE SPIRIT

So, if we live in the environment of God's circumambient Spirit, sharing in God's family and in the unfolding drama of God's promises, how are we to live wisely in that reality? What is it to learn wisdom in the Spirit in each of those spheres?

First, a word about wisdom. It is something the Bible tells us to pursue passionately, to value more than wealth, and to get up early to seek (Proverbs, Job etc.). Jesus, says Luke, grew in wisdom (Luke 2:52). I think the best way to sum up what we are doing in theology is that we are seeking the wisdom of God. I spent ten years recently writing a book on Christian wisdom,[3] and one of the main theological results for me was to bring home again and again how vital the Holy Spirit is, and how important it is to seek wisdom in the Spirit. What might that mean for living in God's Spirit, God's family and God's drama?

One basic thing it means is that we do not possess the Spirit. The Spirit is God's gift and always remains God's gift. We ask for the Spirit afresh daily. We open ourselves to the Spirit again and again and again. God can be utterly trusted to be there for us, to hear us and answer us, but not like a slot machine. God's wisdom is what guides the giving of the Spirit in all forms.

---

3   David F. Ford, *Christian Wisdom: Desiring God and Learning in Love* (Cambridge: Cambridge University Press, 2007).

We ask for the Spirit, and everything else for which we ask, in the name of Jesus Christ, which means that our asking is to be aligned with him and his purposes. So the basic Christian wisdom about the Spirit is: cry out for it. 'Come, Holy Spirit!' is the most fundamental prayer, through which all others are shaped. And, as Angela Tilby, the vicar of my church in Cambridge, St Bene't's, said in a group gathered to discuss some of the thoughts that have gone into this paper, 'asking is part of the way the Spirit is given'. Do it, and be open to surprises from a God who often takes our prayers more seriously than we do.

Another basic thing is that each of the three dimensions of circumambient Spirit, God's family and God's drama is inexhaustibly rich. Whatever you understand and say of them, there is always more. This superabundance is a hallmark of things to do with the Spirit. The Spirit is a spring welling up forever, light that shines eternally, wind that blows afresh each day and each night. I think that is why in the Gospel of John such an emphasis is placed on the Spirit as a reminder:

'But the Advocate, the Holy Spirit, whom the Father will send in my name, will teach you everything, and remind you of all that I have said to you.'

John 14:26

Even one or two words (think of 'glory' or 'love' or 'being transformed') can go on having its meaning enriched year after year, let alone one verse [2 Corinthians 4:6], one story, one book, one prayer or one liturgy. A good deal of growth in wisdom in the Spirit is to do with how we find, for example, the Lord's Prayer becoming more and more important as each phrase is filled with further meaning, and the events of our lives resonate with its petitions. Much growth in wisdom in the Spirit comes through how we *re-read*, how we go back again and again to

49

rich texts and slowly enter their depths. So, about God's Spirit, family and drama there is no end to what might be said, but I will confine myself now to one main thought on each, and relate them to the Lord's Prayer. I start with the family.

1. 'Our Father' – all children included

'Our Father in heaven' prays to God from within a family. But who is included in this family? In the light of God's creation of all, and Jesus Christ dying for all, the Christian question is: Who, if any, are excluded? I am fascinated by the uses of 'all' in Scripture, especially those that look to God's future. As Paul wrestles with the rejection by fellow Jews of his gospel message, and with the huge question of who are embraced within God's people, he arrives at an astonishing conclusion: 'For God has imprisoned all in disobedience so that he may be merciful to all' (Romans 11:32).

Then he cries out about the mystery of God in a crescendo that again uses 'all':

O the depth of the riches and wisdom and knowledge of God! How unsearchable are his judgements and how inscrutable his ways! 'For who has known the mind of the Lord? Or who has been his counsellor?' 'Or who has given a gift to him, to receive a gift in return?' For from him and through him and to him are all things. To him be glory forever. Amen.

Romans 11:33–36

Another use of 'all' in close conjunction with the wisdom of God, this time with explicit mention of the Spirit, is in the opening of the letter to the Ephesians:

With all wisdom and insight he has made known to us the mystery of his will, according to his good pleasure that

50

he set forth in Christ, as a plan for the fullness of time, to gather up all things in him, things in heaven and things on earth. In Christ we have also obtained an inheritance, having been destined according to the purpose of him who accomplishes all things according to his counsel and will, so that we, who were the first to set our hope on Christ, might live for the praise of his glory. In him you also, when you had heard the word of truth, the gospel of your salvation, and had believed in him, were marked with the seal of the promised Holy Spirit; this is the pledge of our inheritance toward redemption as God's own people, to the praise of his glory.

Ephesians 1:8–14

So much is happening there – and that is only one part wrenched out of an even richer passage that begins by addressing 'the God and Father of our Lord Jesus Christ' – but it is clear that this Father's wisdom and love encompasses all people. As the letter says later: this is 'the Father, from whom every family in heaven and on earth takes its name' (Ephesians 3:14–15 – What a prayer!) So it would be unwise for us to decide that any are excluded. Who would dare to determine the edge of the Spirit, or the boundary that the Spirit may not cross? We are in a family that we must consider as potentially universal, even if there are all sorts of boundaries that may seem appropriate for now.

Ephesians goes on in the next chapter to give the rationale for this boundary-crossing: there is now 'one new humanity' [*kainos anthropos*] created out of Jews and Gentiles through the peace-making death of Jesus. One image there is of a dividing wall being broken down, creating a new, shared space, one family home for one humanity. And it is worth remembering that, when a wall between two rooms falls down, those who have previously been at the edges, on the margins, are now central.

2. *'Hallowed be your name' – loving God for God's sake*
'Hallowed be your name' is the encompassing petition of the
Lord's Prayer, and it resonates (as do many other aspects of
the Lord's Prayer) with the final prayer of Jesus in John 17.
To read them together as examples of Spirit-led prayer and
theology is to be oriented afresh to God and God's name, God's
circumambient glory, God's holiness. In Jesus, and in all those
saints who reflect him, we see a Spirit attracting us to God for
God's sake. They are not in it for what they can get out of it,
or for some ulterior motive. Loving God for God's sake is the
motive, and it sets them free from domination by any other
motive or desire. This is at the core of the holiness of the Holy
Spirit: the purity of loving God.

This is also at the core of the wisdom of God. The book
of Job is shaped around this wisdom. Job has a reputation as
supremely wise and good, but in chapter 1 Satan asks the critical
question: 'Does Job fear God for nothing?' (Job 1:9). Is Job
in relationship with God for the sake of having wealth, family,
health, reputation, wisdom or religious satisfaction? (Are we?)
When tested to the limits, does Job want God above all? Job
goes on crying out to God through all his sufferings. His friends
offer him neat theological and moral packages, and never face
up to the deep theological questions with which Job challenges
them.

The eventual judgement in favour of Job and against his
friends is a rejection of shallow theology, of theology that just
repeats the past formulae and avoids facing new things God is
doing now. Job is a theologian of faith and courage who insists
on asking the hard questions even when all he finds are further
questions and problems. This is the Spirit in action, questioning
God, complaining to God, exploring all sorts of ways of
understanding God and God's ways, stretching the mind and
imagination, leading to truth through weakness and suffering,

overwhelmed by the mystery of creation and of God. It is Job the faithful and daring theologian who is vindicated, not his friends with their answers that have everything wrapped up.

And it is all for the sake of a 'for nothing' relationship with God, a relationship in which Job freely relates to God because God is supremely worth relating to. And what about God? Might this not also be the deepest desire of God, that we human beings relate to him in freedom and in wisdom – out of pure love? The joy of such a relationship, delight in the other for the other's sake, which can also be tasted at times in our relationships with each other, might be the deep secret of creation, a secret that is the mystery of the relationship between Jesus and his Father through crucifixion and resurrection.

3. 'Your kingdom come' – discernment of cries
Then there is the drama of the coming of God's kingdom: 'Your kingdom come.' Kelsey's book *Eccentric Existence* has some of the best thinking I know on the Christian challenge of living at a time when the crucifixion and resurrection of Jesus, together with the coming of the Holy Spirit at Pentecost, have inaugurated God's kingdom but it is not yet completed. We are right to be joyful and hopeful, but we also must be realistic about evil, sin and all those forces that resist God and God's good purposes, and that hold people and institutions in bondage. We live in a deeply ambiguous world, in which there are momentous struggles and conflicts. But the past is not simply determinative; God's future, God's Spirit, is given in the present, so there can be fresh starts, new life, a new creation, transformations, signs of the kingdom of God. All the social, economic and cultural powers are the concern of the Spirit of God, and there are strong tensions between the old and the new. They are all relativised and judged, but also blessed with the promise of God, who is drawing them to their consummation in his kingdom.

In that drama, our roles are not divine. We are not the bearers of history, we are not responsible for its consummation. So what is our responsibility? First, to wait on God. Christian spirituality offers many disciplines of radical receptivity, whether in silence (from the tradition of contemplative prayer to Quaker worship), or in keeping the Sabbath both literally and through other practices of quietness, rest and trust in God – God not only works while we sleep, but God too rests. Second, to seek God's wisdom. Kelsey's lengthy discussion of Christian living in the light of God's promises is one of the best – I would place it alongside that of Dietrich Bonhoeffer in his *Ethics* – on the relation between the ultimate and penultimate. But I have one further key thought about that wisdom.

As we participate daily in the drama, we are surrounded by cries. There are cries of suffering above all, but also of joy, wonder, thanks, praise, victory, defeat, fear, faith, despair, and much else. Some of the cries come through the media, some from people and groups we know well, and some come from inside ourselves, perhaps springing from traumas and miseries of our past. Our task is the discernment of these cries. How our lives as communities and individuals are shaped depends crucially on this discernment. Wisdom is about the discernment of cries. Can we hear them in the Spirit? Can we discern our calling in relation to them? Can we relate them to the cries and promises of God?

This is a risky business, and there are no simple formulae. We think of Luke's account of Jesus at the beginning of his ministry. He is full of the Holy Spirit after his baptism, and then faces temptation in the wilderness. Each temptation is a deeply attractive appeal and he discerns the response to each with the help of Scripture. Then he begins his ministry by quoting Isaiah:

'The Spirit of the Lord is upon me, because he has anointed me to bring good news to the poor. He has sent me to

proclaim release to the captives and recovery of sight to the blind, to let the oppressed go free, to proclaim the year of the Lord's favour.'

Luke 4:18–19

The Spirit is upon him to respond to cries, and his calling is discerned through Scripture. My point is that in the drama of the coming of God's kingdom we too are called to attend to the cries of our world and discern our response with the help of Scripture. Scripture is full of cries – from God, from people, even from creation. The book of Job is one of the most intense sets of cries. The climactic book of the Bible, Revelation, is perhaps the noisiest of all. Reading Scripture in the Spirit allows such cries to resonate with those of our world and of our own hearts, and to discern how God is drawing us into his kingdom now.

I think here of Jean Vanier, founder of the L'Arche communities where those with and without mental disabilities live together. At the origin of his life's work he was responding to the cries of those he found shut away in institutions, forgotten and unloved. I think too of politicians. One might see every department of government representing a basic cry – for education, security, justice, housing, wealth, health and so on. The critical task of wisdom is to discern priorities and appropriate responses. And in each of our lives there are competing claims on our attention, time, energy and resources: How can our judgements and commitments be in line with the coming of God's kingdom?

GIVING SIGNS

But discernment of cries is not enough: How do we respond to them in the Spirit? The final part of my chapter, giving signs, is one way into this vital question.

In order to inaugurate the kingdom of God Jesus did not give into the temptation to have royal power over all the kingdoms of the world. Instead he gave signs of his kingdom: teachings, parables, prophecies, healings, exorcisms, forgiving sins, befriending the marginal, gathering a group of disciples. Even more importantly, he himself became a sign, above all in what happened to him, his suffering, death and resurrection. The one who was filled with the Spirit went the way of the cross, and in this way the power of the Spirit was redefined. It is a power that works through weakness and vulnerability and yet is ultimately unconquerable. So the sign of the cross has become the central mark of Christian identity in baptism, and on the night before he died Jesus gave another rich sign centred on his death, the Lord's Supper, Holy Communion, Eucharist or Mass.

We recognise the work of the Spirit as we are drawn more and more deeply into these signs – our baptism, the Eucharist, and especially the scriptural testimony to the signs Jesus gave and the sign he was and is. Traditionally, that is at the heart of how the Spirit is present – through word and sacrament. Bonhoeffer suggests we add a third basic sign, that of community, what I have been discussing as God's family. All three came together beautifully in St Bene't's Church in Cambridge recently. A Chinese student, Shufan, had come into Christian faith undramatically over some time and gone through some months of catechesis. And there she was, quietly radiant, making the promises, being baptised and confirmed, receiving the sign of the cross, taking the bread and wine, and being welcomed into the church community. As we identify with such signs, we too can be inspired to recognise and give signs of God and God's kingdom, and even to be signs. Here we return to the superabundance of particulars and the glorious, endless diversity that I spoke about at the beginning.

We all give signs and are signs all the time, but signs of what? Life in the Spirit involves giving and being signs of the kingdom of God, signs of the good purposes of God for all humanity and creation. These signs are mostly small parts of everyday life, the words and acts of faith, love, understanding, compassion and hope. Some are long term, like a marriage, a friendship, building up an organisation, or the whole shape of a life. Others are one-off events or actions. Some are interior and hidden. Others are more public or at least between two people or a group. And part of the generativity of the Spirit is that signs give rise to more signs, above all in testimonies and in gratitude and praise to God.

I want to conclude by choosing, out of thousands of possibilities, four particular signs of the Spirit drawing us into the kingdom of God, for which I am grateful.

1. Speaking in tongues
First, there is the practice of speaking in tongues. The primary theological description given by Paul in 1 Corinthians 12–14 is that speaking in tongues is addressed to God and conveys 'mysteries in the Spirit'. As practised in the Pentecostal and charismatic movements since the beginning of the twentieth century, it is a form of prayer, praise, blessing, thanksgiving, an outpouring of sounds that can be sung or said. It is a little gift, which Paul exercised and recognised that not all Christians are given, but he hoped that all might have it.

It is both radically intimate, between the speaker and God, and also can be practised in and by groups. It is therefore a sign that has that doubleness of intimacy and publicity seen in the giving of the Spirit in John and in the Acts of the Apostles. Further, it might be seen as a 'pure cry', a calling out to God whose content even the caller does not know, but which can express joy, wonder, anguish, grief and much else.

Sadly (in my judgement), speaking in tongues has been caught up in many fruitless disputes, such as whether it is a necessary mark of having received the Holy Spirit (on that, I think there is no doubt that the biblical case is very weak). A little gift of freedom with the tongue, meant to build up the church, has been turned into an instrument of exclusion or even superiority. It should be possible for *both* those who speak in tongues *and* for those who do not to delight in it and to praise God together as Christians.

One of my colleagues when I was in the University of Birmingham was the distinguished scholar of Pentecostalism, Professor Walter Hollenweger. An image he used for speaking in tongues was 'a cathedral of sound'. Those who usually do not have cathedrals of stone but might be worshipping in tin huts or the open air, can, especially through singing in tongues together, create an inspiring circumambient sound. And not everyone who worships within that cathedral of sound needs to have the gift of tongues.

Hollenweger's vivid image is an invitation to the theological imagination. The meaning of tongues is wonderfully underdetermined. Scripture says almost nothing about it, but does promise that the Spirit will lead into all the truth (John 16:13). So how might this practice that plays a part in the worship and lives of hundreds of millions of Christians be further imagined as a sign of life in God's kingdom? I will just list a few possibilities to set you thinking.

- Abstract speech, on the analogy of abstract art – not representational, letting the tongue 'paint in sounds', often conveying great intensity.

- Superabundant speech – a luxuriant overflow of praise towards God, yet with a strongly apophatic dimension – only God knows what is being said.

- A sabbath of speech – when the tongue takes a holiday from natural language and relaxes into a flow of sounds that one does not have to work at but directs solely to God.

- A sacrament of speech – a sign of intimacy with God that 'effects what it signifies' – and raising questions about how it functions in different Christian traditions, especially those that are strongly sacramental.

- A dance of the tongue – this is the tongue 'dancing' before God, playing freely without worrying about the formal dance steps of natural language.

- Baby talk – regression to being infants of God, able to play with sounds and have the types of speech that go on with babies, often mixing sense and nonsense in expressive, affectively powerful and linguistically improvisatory ways.

- Speech of the mentally disabled – the experience of being at a meal in a L'Arche community has parallels to hearing tongues.

- The prolific near-chaos and non-order in nature – when I was in Rwanda recently, tracking gorillas through tropical rainforest, the sheer abundance of the vegetation was like a visual version of the sound of tongues.

- A language of resistance – the free speech of the largest self-organised movement of poor people today (Pentecostalism).[4]

The analogies could continue endlessly, reinforcing the rich under-determination of the practice. Clearly glossolalia can have an immense variety of meanings in different contexts,

4 On this and on the whole phenomenon of speaking in tongues, one of the most perceptive recent works is *Speaking in Tongues: Multi-disciplinary Perspectives*, Mark J. Cartledge (ed.) (Milton Keynes and Waynesboro, GA: Paternoster Press, 2006).

and this vagueness makes it not only highly adaptable but also manipulable. It is a sign of the Holy Spirit in its risks as well as its possibilities for good, and it is worth noting how threatening it can be to certain forms of order (whether in an individual personality, a church community, or a civil or political community) to try to cope with something that can be so abundant, free, uncontainable, incomprehensible and hard to categorise or control.

2. Worship after genocide

The second sign is a worship service I attended in Rwanda. It took place in Solace Ministries, a genocide survivors' centre in Kigali. My daughter Rebecca had done fieldwork there for her dissertation in social anthropology and they had invited her and her family back for Christmas. So our family of five lived there with people who had survived the 1994 genocide in which a million people died. Their stories, and visiting genocide sites and memorials, were an immersion in horror and trauma whose effects were still tangible.

To enter into all that is beyond the scope of this chapter; here I simply want to give a brief account of worship on our last Sunday. There were about 700 people there, and the service lasted about six and a half hours. It included moving testimonies by survivors who had witnessed families being wiped out, horrendous murder, rape, torture and humiliation, and had often suffered appallingly themselves. There were also testimonies of recovery, healing, salvation, compassion and renewed life.

One whole side of the hall where we were gathered was filled with surviving widows, most of whom had lost children as well as husbands, and the majority were infected with HIV AIDS as a result of being raped. There was a lively music group of singers and instruments, and enthusiastic praise. Then, after the testimonies, a dance group from another survivors' centre entered in local costume. They danced to the drums, stamping vigorously, joyfully. Some were old enough to have been through the genocide – like children the widows had lost. Some were too young to have been through it – children the widows could never have. As the dancers came into the centre, the widows suddenly, almost as a group, broke down in tears, weeping and wailing. Grief and joy went together, simultaneously, intensely. It was like crucifixion and resurrection together. But it was also clear that they were not equally balanced; the dancing meant that the genocide did not have the last word – it was a sign of the Spirit of Jesus Christ.

3. Pee-pee et caca

Third, there is an organisation, the Federation of L'Arche Communities. I have already referred to Jean Vanier's life in response to the cry of those with mental disabilities. The spirit of L'Arche was illustrated by a recent conversation between Jean Vanier and Frances Young, a scholar and theologian whose son, Arthur, is severely disabled, both mentally and physically. The conversation was about the Holy Spirit in ordinary life, and Frances reflected on changing the nappies of Arthur, now in his forties, every day. Jean said: '*Oui, pee-pee et caca!*' Somehow, the Holy Spirit linked to cleaning up the '*pee-pee et caca*' of those who cannot do it for themselves seems a fitting image of living in the Spirit in a very messy world.

4. Jazz

Finally, there is jazz. Springing from Afro-Americans with a history of slavery, it has something of the suffering and joy together of that Rwandan worship – what the title of the classic little book by Wynton Marsalis and Carl Vigeland calls *Jazz in the Bittersweet Blues of Life.*[5] There are many other resonances

---

5 Cambridge, MA: Da Capo Press, 2001.

with the Holy Spirit: continual creativity of improvisation and a sense of abundant outpouring with the thrill of surprise; intense community among players who need to be utterly attentive to what the others are doing, trusting each other, taking risks, and constantly exercising self-discipline in the interests of the whole performance; freedom in playing that comes from years of faithful practice and intimate knowledge of instruments and themes; simultaneity of alert receptivity and energetic activity; the combination of utter realism with 'grace to soar'; and promise of a better future. All those come together in 'Flightline' by the poet Micheal O'Siadhail:

At the core of all the jazz's lavish promise
Just to keep on playing, to improvise what is.

Saxman Keith Donald told me when the solo moves
It's loose and certain as the promise of loves.

'I'd know,' he said, 'the true line after one bar,
As if trusting one another we'll play what we are.'

Those riffs forgone, adornments you had to eschew,
The siren's sweetness that wails so deep in you,

Between moments endured and moments of the dream,
Singleness of purpose, utter obedience to a theme.

Nothing show-off. Lean flightlines. Grace to soar.
Shaping and shaped by a promise at the music's core.[6]

---

6 Micheal O'Siadhail, *Flightline* (Bloodaxe Books, 1998), Reproduced by permission.

This is Wynton Marsalis's earthy way of saying something similar:

You don't necessarily learn about jazz in school. Many folks have this idea that jazz means you're up there on the bandstand playing whatever comes into your head, and hopefully when you're done the other cats will be about done too. It isn't like that at all. Jazz improvisation is the creation of blues-based melodies in the context of harmonic, rhythmic, and timbral variation. There's a logic to its imposition of order on what would otherwise be chaos. And we all create the logic as we go along. The most important emotion in jazz is joy. But you don't create that joy just by feeling good. You create it by feeling terrible. Worse than that. About all the bullshit that has been put on people and continues to be heaped on. You have an empathy, a desire to improve things, to say stuff can be another way, not just about black people but the spiritual condition of all people. You've got to play. Together. You can't play jazz alone.[7]

The Spirit too has its logic – the Spirit's core emotion is joy inseparable from suffering and a passion for the flourishing of all people, and above all it shapes the 'together' of love.

---

7 Marsalis and Vigeland, *op. cit*, p.167.

63

4   THE HOLY SPIRIT IN THE BIBLE

ROWAN WILLIAMS

I will begin this chapter by citing two texts from Romans 8, one of the great texts on the Holy Spirit in Scripture.

First of all, Romans 8:14–16:

*For all who are led by the Spirit of God are children of God.
For you did not receive a Spirit of slavery to fall back into
fear, but you have received a spirit of adoption. When we
cry, 'Abba! Father!' it is that very Spirit bearing witness
with our Spirit that we are children of God. ...[NRSV]*

And then Romans 8:22–26:

*For we know that up to the present time all of creation
groans with pain, like the pain of childbirth. But it is not just
creation alone which groans: we who have the Spirit as the
first of God's gifts also groan within ourselves as we wait for
God to make us his children and set our whole being free.
For it was by hope that we were saved; but if we see what
we hope for, then it's not really hope. For who of us hopes
for something we see? But if we hope for what we do not see,*

we wait for it with patience. In the same way, the Spirit also comes to help us, weak as we are. For we do not know how we ought to pray; the Spirit himself pleads with God for us in groans that words cannot express.

Hope is often for us in everyday usage a slightly weak word, 'I hope it won't rain tomorrow', 'I hope I've got that right', 'I hope I'm making sense', but 'hope' here in Romans 8 is something much deeper and much more passionate. This chapter of Paul's letter to the Romans is about longing, and that's where I want to begin: the Spirit's association not simply with hope in that rather minimal, rather Anglican sense, but hope as earnest, energetic longing, yearning. So that to speak of the Spirit's presence in the church is to speak of that dimension of the life of Christ's body that is consumed with longing.

At the heart of the church, there is a yearning to be what God designs us to be, a yearning to receive the full gifts that God wants us to receive – and that carries with it the implication that there is indeed something that we are for. Human beings are not just random, they're for something, there is a kind of magnetic needle quivering in there somewhere, pointing to the north, and when our hearts are engaged in and through Jesus Christ, what happens is that that magnetic drive comes to life, that yearning is kindled. The Spirit in us is God pressing us towards what we are made for.

This came home to me very vividly when I was reminded quite recently of a text from a very ancient writer from another part of the Christian world. This is from St Simeon, a Greek Orthodox writer of little over 1,000 years ago. Here is his prayer to the Holy Spirit:

Come, you who have become desire in me, you who have wanted me to desire the unreachable you.

Come, you who have become desire in me and have wanted me to desire the unreachable you.

There's the restlessness, there's the yearning in the heart of Christian identity. The Spirit in us is desire, not any old desire, but the desire towards the unreachable God, who is also the God who has himself reached out to us and put the Spirit of his Son into our hearts.

Yes, we groan wordlessly in our yearning, but those wordless sighs, that almost desperate longing that we can't find words for is, St Paul tells us, caught in, embodied in that one, simple, all-embracing prayer of Jesus Christ himself, 'Abba, Father.' So the desire, the yearning that the Spirit puts in us, could also be seen simply as the desire to be where Jesus Christ is, because when we are where he is, praying with his prayer, then we're at home, then we're human.

God purposes us to be his children. God's design is for us to desire to be where Jesus is and when we are there, praying in that confidence, that almost terrified confidence, projected into this astonishing place and yet knowing it's the place we ought to be, when that happens we are expressing what was supposed to be. We yearn to be where Christ is, we pray Christ's prayer hoping that the Spirit cumulatively, day-by-day, moves us that bit further towards that place.

But, of course, children grow. To desire to be the child of God is not to desire to be childish, to curl up in silence and passivity with God and be cuddled to sleep. The good – or possibly bad – news is that to be God's child is to be God's growing child, growing into Jesus and therefore growing into the extraordinary fact of Jesus' self-offering. Where does Jesus pray 'Abba, Father'? In the garden of Gethsemane. Jesus prays his Spirit-filled prayer in a place where all his powers of will and resolve and courage and fidelity are summoned up in order to accept

God's will for the salvation of the world. Jesus prays 'Abba, Father' in the moment of his deepest darkness, a darkness of soul and mind and imagination. Jesus prays 'Abba, Father' at the point where the longing to be with his Father is something that has to sweep through and sweep away all thought of self-protection or self-service.

So we really ought to be rather careful when we pray, 'Abba, Father', because which of us could put our hands on our hearts and say where we yearn to be is in the garden of Gethsemane? Not I, and probably not you! And yet, mysteriously, the power, the energy, the desire of the Holy Spirit is to take us there, because growing into Christ's self-offering is what the gift of Christ means.

And our longing for God, therefore, kindled by the Spirit, our longing to be where Jesus is, is a longing to be where the protections, the walls around myself, fall away, where entering into Christ I can let go of what keeps my boundaries safe, and simply be taken into the stream of healing love that flows from the Father.

Put like that, of course, the temptation is simply to look within ourselves, hear the Holy Spirit, uttering that great prayer of longing and say 'Stop it, I don't really want to be there at all.' And perhaps that's what St Paul meant in another place by quenching the Spirit. Perhaps the real quenching of the Spirit is the trying to sit hard on that frightening yearning and energy to be where Christ is, as we begin to wake up to what it is that we have signed up to.

So the Holy Spirit in us is in every sense the Spirit of passion, the Spirit of Christ's passion and the Spirit of yearning and longing love within us. And if that's the gift of the Spirit in the church, then we begin to see in outline some of what we might want to say to our contemporary world. In Romans 8, St Paul writes about freedom, and the first thing we would want to say

67

in the light of all this is that true freedom is freedom for full humanity. And immediately following on from that, of course, we want to say full humanity is Christ-shaped.

And then comes this difficult and challenging moment when we begin to see what that implies. Freedom is freedom for full humanity, full humanity is Christ-shaped, and so, thirdly, freedom is what theologians call 'kenotic': it is freedom for self-emptying. 'Let this mind be in you which was also in Christ Jesus', as we read in Philippians 2:5 [NKJV]. A full humanity is not a humanity that is blithely or blandly in control, but a humanity that is overwhelmed by the energy of giving, with all the recklessness and the risk that that entails.

But the fourth and very significant point is to say that although our freedom is kenotic, self-emptying, self-forgetting, it mysteriously combines with the intense aliveness of longing that is in us in and through all this. Being self-forgetting and self-giving does not mean being passive – it means letting your action and God's be so blended together that the energy of giving is what defines you. And that is being fully alive, that is God's Spirit and our spirit winding themselves together, as Paul tells us in Romans 8.

Freedom for a fuller humanity; fuller humanity is Christ-shaped; Christ-shaped means self-emptying and self-emptying means being filled with the energy of gift and being fully alive. So this freedom becomes a passion, not for gratification or comfort or security, it becomes a passion for God and a passion for God's world. If the Spirit has become desire in me, the Spirit has also become desire, hunger for God's justice, God's righteousness. Our Lord speaks in the Beatitudes of a hunger and thirst for righteousness.

That is summed up very powerfully in a phrase from an extraordinary figure again from the Christian East: Mother Maria Skobtsova, a Russian nun who lived in Paris in the

1930s, worked with refugees, and who became more and more consumed with work, particularly with Jewish refugees. She and her tiny community in Paris worked to defend first of all the poor in Paris and then particularly the Jews of that city when the Nazis arrived in the early 1940s. She herself was eventually arrested and ended her life in Ravensbrück concentration camp on Good Friday in 1945, where she stepped forward to volunteer to substitute for another woman who was about to be taken to the gas chamber.

Mother Maria had a very bumpy and difficult life – she was not anything like a plaster saint. She was a single mother, divorced, attempting to bring up a couple of children in Paris in very poor circumstances. She decided, against the advice of a great many people, to take monastic vows because she wanted to give everything to God in service, in passion. She remained a highly unconventional nun: apparently her neighbours used to complain about the noise from her rooms late at night because so many people would come in for parties.

But during those years when she was trying to discern what God was calling her to do, she wrote these words: 'Either Christianity is fire or there is no such thing.' What a perfect summary of the sense of the Holy Spirit becoming desire in us, a desire not for religious feelings, not for religious safety, but a desire to be a place where God's own passion comes through and is at home.

So connecting this to our subject of the Holy Spirit in the world today, perhaps it is beginning to come into focus that what we're really talking about when we're talking about the Holy Spirit is true and false humanity. Living in the Spirit and understanding what the Spirit is about is understanding something about being human that is so extraordinary and profound, radical and shocking that we really do have something to talk about when we're out there in our present cultural arguments. The Spirit in the world today is about humanity in the world today and you could say that the Christian church overall is – or ought to be – a sort of campaign for real humanity, like the campaign for real ale.

Real human beings are, of course, a bit of an endangered species. The Holy Spirit is about the choices we make as to what we think is human. Today more than ever, there are very fundamental choices about what it means to be human, and many, many people are trying desperately to raise these questions. They need permission to ask them more loudly, more consistently and more audibly in the public sphere.

What is really human? Is it the fantasies of control, of unbridled, unsystematised desire; is it the longing for safety and satisfaction? Is being really human being free from the constraints of one another's needs? Is being really human being always in charge of every moment of my life right up to the moment, the chosen moment of my death? Or is it something else?

Believing in the Holy Spirit suggests indeed that it is something else. The humanity brought alive by the Holy Spirit is a humanity that is mortal and bodily and limited and dependent. It is a humanity we discover together. The humanity created by the Holy Spirit is a life which is held together, not by my will to succeed or control, but by God's passion, God's desire for me turned into my desire for God. It is a life held together by that longing to be transformed into the active, endless love of the Father and the Son.

And that's a humanity that does not break down into powerful and powerless, rich and poor; it is a humanity in which everybody's poverty and need is affirmed and recognised; everybody's need of one another is recognised. It is a humanity in which we look for that needle, that quivering magnetic needle of yearning towards what we are meant to be, what we are made to be. Not a humanity trying to escape, a humanity that says 'We've arrived or we'll arrive very soon at a state where we no longer need passion or desire', but rather a humanity always opening out onto the endlessness of God. And that humanity comes to birth not by our skill, not by our unaided virtue, not by our success: that humanity comes to birth in the daily renewal of our prayer as we say 'Abba, Father', as we live in hope, yearning hope, longing hope, for the transfiguration of all things.

So I conclude this chapter by taking you back to where we began: Romans 8, this time verses 26–31:

In the same way, the Spirit also comes to help us, weak as we are. For we do not know how we ought to pray; the Spirit himself pleads with God for us in groans that words cannot express. And God, who sees into our hearts, knows what the thought of the Spirit is; because the Spirit pleads with God on behalf of his people and in accordance with his will. We know that in all things God works for good with those who love him, those whom he has called according to his purpose. Those whom God had already chosen, he also set apart to become like his Son, so that the Son would be the first among many believers. And so, those whom God set apart, he called; and those he called, he put right with himself, and he shared his glory with them. In view of all this, what can we say? If God is for us, who can be against us?

5 LIFE IN THE SPIRIT: IDENTITY, VOCATION AND THE CROSS OF CHRIST[1]

GRAHAM TOMLIN

Who am I? And what am I here for? These are two of the most basic questions that people ask. They can receive religious answers of course, but they are not just religious questions – they are also universal ones. Everyone asks them at some time or other. This chapter shows how pneumatology can begin to help provide answers to these two questions, not just in an abstract fashion, but also in an existential way.

The starting point for these reflections is the work of the artist Charlie Mackesy.[2]Mackesy is fascinated by the story of the prodigal son (Luke 15:11–32), and in particular the moment in the story when the son returns to be embraced by his father. In a number of paintings and bronze sculptures he depicts this moment. The image works on two levels.

On the first, it captures the moment in the story when the father embraces the son after his return from the far country. It

---

1 A fuller version of the material in this chapter can be found in G. Tomlin, *The Prodigal Spirit: The Trinity, the Church and the Future of the World* (London: SPTC, 2011)
2 http://www.charliemackesy.com/

vividly conveys the pathos of the embrace, the emotional power of reconciliation. On another level, particularly when viewed by a Christian onlooker, it depicts the lost sinner returning to God. Many people have found these sculptures and paintings express very powerfully their own sense of having been welcomed back into the presence and embrace of God the Father after many years in the metaphorical and spiritual wilderness: the 'son' in the image is not the prodigal son of Jesus' story – it is me. It conveys that sense of 'coming home', of being picked up again in the warmth of the Father's love.

Perhaps, however, there is also a third level on which the image works: as a window into the life of the Trinity. From this perspective, it depicts God the Father's love for God the Son. The Son in the image is lifeless, hanging limp and helpless in the Father's arms, while the Father embraces him with wide-eyed passion and a hint of agony in his face. Viewed as a depiction of the relationship between the Son and the Father, it focuses on the embrace by the Father of the dead Son, the Son who has given his life in the sacrifice of the cross. It is a kind of *Pietà*, although this time not of Mary cradling her dead son in her arms, but in a deeper theological sense, it is the Father who catches up the dead Son in his arms, and in so doing brings him to life again. In the parable of the prodigal son in Luke's Gospel, the line, 'For this son of mine was dead and is alive again' (Luke 15:24) makes an intriguing connection to the death and resurrection of the Son.

As a window into the life of the Trinitarian relations however, it seems to lack one important dimension: the Holy Spirit. This is where we return to the second level on which the image works – the one where the viewer is drawn into the picture to identify with the embraced son. This begins to highlight the role of the Spirit – to draw us into the love between the Father and the Son.

Two passages from the New Testament help to draw this out. The first comes from Luke 3. At the baptism of Jesus, the Father sends the Spirit onto the Son in one of the great Trinitarian moments of the Gospels. The Father's words are significant: 'You are my Son, whom I love; with you I am well pleased' (Luke 3:22). This statement immediately locates Jesus' identity at the outset of his ministry: he is not just the Son, but he is the *beloved* Son of the Father. Being a son or daughter of course does not guarantee that one is beloved – not all children know themselves as the beloved children of their parents. But this Son is identified first and foremost as the primary object of the love of the Father. The bond between the Father and the Son is one not of disapproval or disappointment or even expectation or hope – it is love.

In John's Gospel, no voice is heard in the baptism story, however the whole Gospel might be seen as an exploration of the theme of the love of the Father for the Son. The phrase 'the Father loves the Son' is repeated several times in a way that adds an extra dimension to this love – the note of trust: 'The Father loves the Son and has placed everything in his hands' (John 3:35); and: 'For the Father loves the Son and shows him all he does ... Moreover, the Father judges no one, but has entrusted all judgement to the Son' (John 5:20–22). The Son is the one to whom the Father alone entrusts judgement. The deep security and peace of the figure of Christ in the Gospels comes from this profound sense of trust, the knowledge of the Father's love: it is the secret of his identity.

The second passage comes from Romans 8:15–17:

You received the Spirit of sonship. And by him we cry, Abba, Father. The Spirit himself testifies with our spirit that we are God's children. Now if we are children, then we are heirs— heirs of God and co-heirs with Christ, if indeed we share in his sufferings in order that we may also share in his glory.

In other words, the Holy Spirit draws us into the same relationship with the Father as Jesus himself has. We are enabled to use the same intimate term of address: Abba. Our relationship with the Father is determined by Jesus' relationship with the Father. Our 'sonship' is not parallel to, or separate from that of Jesus: it is only by virtue of being 'in Christ', as Paul puts it elsewhere, that we are sons and daughters of the Father at all. Naturally, classic Christian theology would insist that there is one crucial difference between our 'sonship' and his – he is the Son by nature, and we are sons and daughters by grace, or adoption (Romans 8:15, 23; 9:4; Galatians 4:5; Ephesians 1:5). However the point is that we are not co-opted as partners but adopted as children, adopted into the same relationship with the Father as the one true Son has.

To put this plainly, the Holy Spirit unites us with Christ so that we can know the love of the Father for the Son, not just objectively acknowledged, but subjectively experienced by our being brought into Christ.

The Holy Spirit is a 'person' in a different sense from the other two persons of the Trinity. The New Testament never claims that the Father loves the Spirit, or that the Son loves the Spirit. This is presumably not because the Spirit is unloved by the other two persons: it is more that the role of the Spirit within the Trinity is different.

St Augustine of course famously described the Spirit as the bond of love between the Father and the Son. This has led to the critique of his Trinitarian theology as suggesting that the two main parts of God are Father and Son, with the Spirit as just a divine substance that binds them together, or that the Spirit is the impersonal 'divinity' that holds them together.[3] It can seem

---

3 See for example G. D. Badcock, *Light of Truth and Fire of Love: A Theology of the Holy Spirit* (Grand Rapids, MI: Eerdmans, 1997), chapter 3.

that the Spirit in this sense is less than personal, a passive 'bond' rather than an active person.

This implied subordination of the Spirit to the Father and the Son, which reached its focus in the later *filioque* controversy, has often led Eastern critics to accuse Western theology of imagining a Spirit who is impersonal, passive and inferior. However, this notion of the Spirit as the bond of love between Father and Son loses its sense of passivity or subordination when the Spirit is seen as actively proceeding from the Father to draw us into the love that exists between the Father and the Son. This is a vibrant, active, alive Spirit who welcomes us into the act of divine hospitality that beats at the heart of the universe. This is clearly the sense meant by Calvin when he describes a similar idea: 'The Holy Spirit is the bond by which Christ effectually unites us to himself ... he unites himself to us by the Spirit alone'.[4] Both Augustine and Calvin help us to see a vital principle, that we should never separate pneumatology from Christology: the Holy Spirit is not some generalised Hegelian *Zeitgeist* or an impersonal spiritual force, but is the Spirit of Christ.

Now all this leads to a number of important insights and implications. First, it helps us understand something of what Christians mean when they speak of the love of God. The statement 'God is love' is of course at the heart of the Christian understanding of God. More precisely however, it is the love of the Father for the Son that is being described. This is the ultimate reality that lies at the heart of all things: the love of the Father for the Son. The Son is, strictly speaking, the only one worthy of the divine love. And he is the true object of the Father's love: if we want to know what kind of thing or person the Father loves, the answer is found in the Son.

---

4   John Calvin, *Institutes*, III.1 and III.3.

The closest analogy we have for this love at the heart of God is the love of a parent for a child, rather than erotic love or the love of friendship. This is perhaps because parental love is love at its most pure, where the bond is deeper than a shared sense of humour, interests or mutual attraction. Children and parents are bound together by a relation so profound that it cannot be sundered even by any decision to part. These relationships can be strained, but they cannot be dissolved. Even a disowned daughter remains a daughter. The love of a parent for a child is also the only love we experience that is not grounded in anything in the beloved. A mother loves her newborn child, not because they can do anything for her, or because of any intrinsic beauty they possess, but simply because they are her child.

'EXPERIENCE' OF THE SPIRIT

Moreover, this suggests a meaning and content to the work of God through the Holy Spirit. Experiences of the Spirit are often spoken of in terms of 'power', or manifest themselves for example in dramatic experiences of healing. When love is seen as the primary category of the Spirit's work, drawing us into the bond between the Father and the Son, then we can see the precise nature of such power. Love is the most powerful force there is, capable of dissolving hatreds, animosities and long-encrusted grievances. Likewise, love is also the most healing force in the world, capable of healing hurt minds, souls and even bodies. Perhaps divine healing should be seen as the result of being embraced in the Son by the Father in the power of the Spirit?

A comparison between two theologians of the Spirit perhaps helps to make the point here. Jonathan Edwards says that the mark of a genuine act of God is the turning of an impersonal knowledge about God into a deeply personal love for him. The believer finds an appetite for God, a 'certain divine spiritual taste' that did not exist before.[5] Edwards' argument is essentially an aesthetic one: faith brings about an ability to see beauty in God, finding him desirable and pleasing, rather than distant or forbidding, or non-existent as he may have seemed before. Edwards knows that a true *love* for God cannot be generated by reason or moral effort: it can only arise through the work of the Spirit.

Friedrich Schleiermacher, however, takes a different approach. Aware of contemporary attacks from the followers of Kant and Locke on the possibility of direct experience of God, he sees religious experience as not actually experience of God at all, but rather a particular way of looking at the world. It is a 'sense of the infinite' or an 'intuition of the universe'. Everyone experiences this 'feeling of absolute dependence', and some interpret this as 'God-consciousness'. In other words, the experience is universal – an experience of infinity.[6] No special capacity is needed to know this dependence, you only need to understand that experience differently: what makes the experience religious is not the experience itself, but the way in which you interpret it.

Edwards however thinks of a 'spiritual sense' – a new form of perception. Both believers and unbelievers have notions of God, however only believers grasp the 'divine excellency', and this is not just a different way of interpreting experience, but a completely new ability to perceive the divine glory, holiness or beauty. These qualities are objective qualities of God, but they are only accessible to the saints by the light of the Holy Spirit. This is not just a different way of looking at things, a different interpretation of a common experience accessible to all, as it is for Schleiermacher. For all Schleiermacher's emphasis on 'feeling' and 'intuition', the main difference between the believer

---

5   J. Edwards, *The Religious Affections* (Edinburgh: Banner of Truth, 1986), p. 185.
6   F. Schleiermacher, *On Religion: Speeches to its Cultured Despisers* (Cambridge: CUP, 1996). The second speech is where this idea is most clearly laid out.

and the unbeliever is essentially conceptual not experiential. They have the same experience: the believer just interprets it differently. For Edwards, there is a more radical difference. The believer has a new ability to perceive the nearness, beauty and holiness of God that the unbeliever does not possess, and this is not just a subjective, private experience, but the apprehension of an objective reality.[7]

Edwards' suggestion helps us define what we mean when we speak, perhaps rather loosely, of 'experiences of the Spirit'. The Spirit enables us to begin to appreciate and experience the love of the Father for the Son, as something personal – a love in which we are included. The Spirit creates in us something new: a capacity to appreciate the beauty and loveliness of God. He opens blind eyes to see what we could not see before, or to change the metaphor, to gain a taste for God.

This is essentially an Augustinian insight. Augustine writes that a person 'receives the Holy Spirit, whereby there arises in his soul the delight in and the love of God, the supreme and changeless Good. This gift is his here and now, while he walks by faith, not yet by sight: that having this as earnest of God's free bounty, he may be fired in heart to cleave to his Creator, kindled in mind to come within the shining of the true light; and thus receive from the source of his being the only true well-being.'[8] This is the work of the Spirit: to draw us into the love

---

7 M. McClymond, *Encounters with God: An Approach to the Theology of Jonathan Edwards* (New York: OUP, 1998), explores the contrast between Edwards and Schleiermacher on this point: 'Edwards clearly would not have accepted Schleiermacher's notion of an implicit awareness of God, that is, a state in which the subject does not recognise God as the object of his or her experience. The mark of genuine spiritual perception is seeing the very "divinity" of God. What also decisively separated Edwards from Schleiermacher and the Romantics generally, was his sharp distinction between the mentality of the regenerate and the unregenerate. For Schleiermacher, the capacity for religious feeling was an intrinsic aspect of human nature per se, and not a special gift that God confers on selected individuals', p. 23.

8 Augustine, 'On the Spirit and the Letter', *Saint Augustine's Anti-Pelagian Writings*, B. B. Warfield (rev.), (Edinburgh: T&T Clark), p. 197.

between the Father and the Son so that we know it as a love in which we are included, not excluded.

IDENTITY

In this way, pneumatology begins to answer the first of the questions posed at the start of this chapter: the question of identity. The answer to the question, 'As a Christian, who am I?' is a fully Trinitarian one. I am a beloved child of the Father because the Spirit unites me with Christ. I therefore can know for myself the same love as the Father has for the Son. I am 'in Christ', embraced by the Father. The love he has for the Son is a love in which I am included by virtue of my being in Christ through faith. It is not just Jesus who can claim the words spoken at his baptism, 'this my beloved son': I can claim them too.

Moreover, we can also know what we shall be. If we are in Christ by the Spirit, then that means being made like the Son. Paul's development of the idea of the Spirit enabling us to enjoy the same filial relationship as Jesus the Son, inevitably ends with this same thought, that 'those God foreknew he also predestined to be conformed to the likeness of his Son, that he might be the firstborn among many brothers and sisters' (Romans 8:29 TNIV). The destiny of those who have been united with the Son so that they begin to know themselves as beloved by the Father is to be conformed to the likeness of Christ.

VOCATION

These insights also help us approach the second of the questions posed at the start: the question of vocation: what are we here for? There is a vital link to be made between creation, Christology and pneumatology. Creation takes place in and through the

Son: 'in him all things in heaven and on earth were created' (Colossians 1:16) [NRSV], 'through him all things were made' (John 1:3). Creation becomes the object of God's love because it was created in and through the Son; it is included and embraced in the love of God the Father because it came into being 'in him'. In other words, it is not just we humans who are included in the embrace between the Father and the Son, but the whole of creation. It came into being in Christ so it, at least potentially, is included in that embrace. As we experience it however, creation, like the prodigal son, has strayed far from that embrace, so that although it came into being in and through the divine love, at present it is 'subjected to frustration' and in 'bondage to decay' (Romans 8:20–21).

Genesis 1:2 has the Spirit brooding over the formless waters as the world is created, and Psalm 104:30 makes the link more explicit: 'When you send your Spirit, they are created, and you renew the face of the earth.' The Holy Spirit is involved in the creative act of God as much as the Son. This connection between creation and pneumatology is developed particularly in patristic theology. Irenaeus writes: 'What could the visible fruit of the invisible Spirit be, if not to make flesh mature and receptive of imperishability ... the Holy Spirit is sent to the entire universe, and since creation, has been transforming it, carrying it towards the final resurrection.'[9]

In the fourth century, St Ambrose described how the Holy Spirit transforms creation from something merely utilitarian and functional to something beautiful:

So when the Spirit was moving upon the water, the creation was without grace; but after this world being created

---

9 Irenaeus, *Against Heresies*, 12.3, in Robert M. Grant (ed.) *Irenaeus of Lyons: The Early Church Fathers* (London: Routledge, 1997), p. 166.

underwent the operation of the Spirit, it gained all the beauty of that grace, wherewith the world is illuminated.[10]

Basil the Great writes of the Spirit's operation on created things: 'He waters them with his life-giving breath and helps them reach their proper fulfilment. He perfects all other things.'[11] As Colin Gunton put it: 'the Spirit is the agent by whom God enables things to become that which they are created to be'.[12] Furthermore, the Spirit also heals creation from its bondage to decay, bringing life and vigour to what is dying or dead. The classic scriptural picture here is that of Ezekiel's valley of the dry bones, where God's breath or Spirit brings the bones together and gives them life.

All of this fills out the picture. The work of the Holy Spirit is to bring all of creation, fully restored and healed, to its fulfilment. It is to draw creation back into the embrace of the Father and the Son. And this gives the vital clue to the question of vocation. Being united with Christ by the Holy Spirit, being increasingly conformed to his image, means being involved in the work of God in Christ through the Spirit, of reconciling the world to God (2 Corinthians 5:18–19). We do this through evangelism, which draws people back into fellowship with God, through medical work and prayer for healing, through striving for the good of all people through legal and, perhaps even sometimes illegal ways. We also do it through Spirit-inspired work that develops the potential of creation through art, technology, the ordering of the world of materials, economies and societies.

---

10 Ambrose, *On the Holy Spirit*, II.V

11 St Basil, 'On the Holy Spirit', 9, in St Basil the Great, *On the Holy Spirit* (Crestwood, New York: St Vladimir's Press, 1980), p. 43.

12 C. Gunton, "The Spirit Moved over the Face of the Waters"; The Holy Spirit and the Created Order' in *Spirit of Truth and Power: Studies in Christian Doctrine and Experience*, David F. Wright (ed.) (Edinburgh; Rutherford House, 2007), 56–72. p. 70.

The Spirit unites us with Christ so that we are drawn into his relationship with the Father, into his healing and perfecting love. The Spirit also unites us with Christ so that we are drawn into his relationship to the world. If the Spirit gives us a new identity by uniting us with Christ as the beloved sons and daughters of the Father, the Spirit also gives us a new vocation, to bring healing, and to elicit the potential of the particular part of creation in which we are placed.

THE SPIRIT AND THE CROSS

Earlier we drew attention to the dimension of the Charlie Mackesy sculpture that showed the Father embracing the crucified and battered Son. To be united with this Christ brings a sobering note to this discussion of vocation. The shape the love of God takes in a fallen world is the cross. This is the passion of God in both senses: God's passionate (fervent) love expresses itself in the passion (suffering) of Christ as he takes on his shoulders the sins of the world. This takes us back to Romans 8: 'The Spirit himself testifies with our spirit that we are God's children. Now if we are children, then we are heirs – heirs of God and co-heirs with Christ, *if indeed we share in his sufferings* in order that we may also share in his glory' (Romans 8:16–17 italics mine).

Sonship involves sharing in the sufferings of the Son as he encounters a world that has run far away from the Father. The Christ who is embraced by the Father is the crucified Christ, the one who gives himself in love for the healing of the world. If we are drawn into Christ by the Spirit, we are drawn both into his personal, powerful knowledge of the love of God and also into his love for the world, which takes the shape of the cross, this is the true *pneumatologia crucis*.

Jürgen Moltmann writes: 'The relation of the Church to the Holy Spirit is the relation of *epiklesis*, continual invocation of the Spirit and unconditional opening for the experiences of the Spirit who confers fellowship and who makes life truly worth living.'[13] A church that regularly invokes the Spirit through the prayer, 'Come Holy Spirit' invites the Spirit to create a new awareness of the love of God, and also a new awareness of the pain of the world and the sufferings of Christ for that world. When that prayer is prayed we should expect powerful manifestations of that love, in episodes of healing, words of prophecy and other tangible signs of God's abiding compassion.

We should also expect to be caught up in the suffering love that reaches out to draw the rest of the world into that healing and maturing love, even when that reaching out is rejected and bruised as Christ was. True life in the Spirit expects both, glories in both. If one is lacking, something authentic about the Spirit's work is missing. When both are present, the Holy Spirit begins to change us and the world around us to reflect the image of Christ, the beloved Son of the Father, which is the goal of all creation.

---

13 Jürgen Moltmann, *The Spirit of Life: A Universal Affirmation* (London: SCM, 1992), p. 230.

6 THE HOLY SPIRIT AND THE REALLY HUMAN JESUS

LINCOLN HARVEY

For Christian theologians, an area of interest often emerges quietly and unannounced. We are busy focusing on a particular field when we begin to sense some really interesting stuff happening elsewhere. It is as if the grass is a little greener nearby. This probably has something to do with what we do. Systematic theology is a skill – the skill of identifying connections, establishing coherence, keeping sight of the whole, saying particular things in due time, yet knowing that everything needs to be said at once, and in concert. Therefore systematic theologians are constantly drawn away from their immediate concern in order to discover how a specific doctrine – variously shaped – will impact its distinct neighbours. And so it came to pass. As I undertook doctoral research on a Trinitarian doctrine of creation, I began to glimpse some interesting stuff out the corner of my eye.[1]

---

1 'All Christian doctrines hang together. They support and inform one another. Starting from any one doctrine you can find your way to all the rest... This is not surprising, since all Christian doctrines are finally about one thing: the charity of the triune God... Remembering and showing the inter-linked nature of doctrine has always been the task of systematic or doctrinal theology; displaying, as it were, its perichoretic relations.' Gerard Loughlin, 'The Basis and Authority of Doctrine' in Colin E. Gunton

Such peripheral vision is often encouraged by a nudge, and my nudge came – with characteristic vigour – from my first supervisor at King's College London, Colin E. Gunton. In a number of conversations, Gunton referred to an unshapely couple: the less human Jesus is understood to be, the less need there is for a full account of the role of the Spirit in the economy of salvation. Or – spun more positively – a proper account of the Spirit's work will run in tandem with a strong account of the genuine humanity of Christ.[2]

My interest provoked, I began to listen in on the seminar discussions attentively.[3] Jesus – though fully divine – was suspected of being portrayed as *too* divine, a move that detracts from his saving human work and renders him of little earthly use today. The over-divinisation of Christ, in turn, creates an economic vacuum which 'plagiarising' mediators fill, claiming as their work *his* ongoing work at the right hand of his Father – a conclusion Douglas Farrow demonstrated convincingly in *Ascension and Ecclesia*.[4] And – as Alan Spence has shown – even when these too-divine Christologies do confess Christ's humanity, the Apollinarian heresy is often at work subtly beneath the camouflage of a misconceived doctrine of the communication of attributes.[5] In practice, the divine Son wields

---

(ed.), *Cambridge Companion to Christian Doctrine* (Cambridge: Cambridge University Press, 1997), p. 52. According to Emil Brunner, the key skill in systematic theology is: 'knowing connections between truths and which belongs to which', so Emil Brunner, *The Mediator: A Study of the Central Doctrine of the Christian Faith* (trans. Olive Wyon) (Philadelphia: Westminster Press, 1947), p. 262.

2 See, for example, Colin E. Gunton, *Theology Through the Theologians* (London and New York: T&T Clark, 1996), p. 153, or Colin E. Gunton, *Christ and Creation: The Didsbury Lectures 1990* (Eugene, Oregon: Wipf & Stock, 2005), p. 50.

3 The main arena for discussion at King's was provided by the weekly seminar of the Research Institute in Systematic Theology, which was followed by less formal discussions over lunch! The seminars continue to be run under the current oversight of Susannah Ticciati.

4 Douglas Farrow, *Ascension and Ecclesia* (Edinburgh: T&T Clark, 1999). Farrow did his doctoral research under Gunton and taught at King's in the 1990s.

5 Alan Spence, 'Christ's Humanity and Ours: John Owen' in Christoph Schwöbel

the humanity like 'an instrument', and the instrument becomes *effectively* divine.

Significantly, there is a knock-on effect. The all-powerful, all-conquering divine agency of the Son – working upon the effectively divinised humanity – renders the Holy Spirit a poor relation in the equation, left rearranging the deckchairs *after* the Titanic Son has pulled the sinking ship back to the surface. In short, the Son does all the important stuff *to* us and the Spirit is rendered subordinate to his crucial work.[6]

However, wanting to rehabilitate God the Spirit within an account of the triune economy, Gunton wondered whether these too-divine Christologies were little more than knee-jerk reactions to the constant threat of the Arian heresy. Overly anxious to say what Arius hadn't wanted, said, Christ's divinity was defensively underlined to such an extent that his genuine humanity was *undermined*. An awkward question therefore presented itself: Had the mainstream tradition somehow got its Christology wrong, misconceiving the work of the Spirit within the reality of incarnate grace?

With this subversive question in mind, I began to notice how discussions at King's would often include mention of a minority position within Christology. This position was often introduced by way of a question: *Was the nature assumed by the Son of God a fallen nature?* For some reason or other, I liked this question

---

and Colin E. Gunton (eds.), *Persons, Divine and Human: King's College Essays in Theological Anthropology* (Edinburgh: T&T Clark, 1991), pp. 74–97. See also the rehearsal of these themes in Alan Spence, *The Promise of Peace: A Unified Theory of Atonement* (London: T&T Clark, 2006), pp. 20–36. Spence was another research student under Gunton. His work influenced Gunton's thinking (and vice versa), as is evidenced, for example, in Colin E. Gunton, *The Promise of Trinitarian Theology*, 2nd edition (London and New York: T&T Clark, 2003), p. 69 and Colin E. Gunton, *Father, Son and Holy Spirit: Toward a Fully Trinitarian Theology* (London and New York: T&T Clark, 2003), p. 99.

6 See Colin E. Gunton, *Theology Through the Theologians* (London and New York: T&T Clark, 1996), pp. 105–128.

(as dangerous as it sounded on first hearing). To my mind, it seemed to connect with a whole host of similar issues, ones which centred on whether or not Jesus was really like us: Did he know what it's like to be caught up in this mess or was the good life somehow easier for him? Had he been some kind of Superman – a different *sort* of humanity from a far away planet – to whom I couldn't really relate? And – if a super-Jesus can't provide a realistic model for my own corrupt life – must I look to the communion of saints for my daily inspiration?

With such questions in mind, the letter to the Hebrews seemed to provide a quarry for further excavation. There, in the second chapter, we read that Christ

> *had to become like his brothers and sisters **in every respect**, so that he might be a merciful and faithful high priest in the service of God ... Because he himself was tested by what he suffered, he is able to help those who are being tested.*[7]

Rapidly drawing a thick line from this 'every respect' straight through to the popular soundbite of Gregory Nazianzus ('the unassumed is the unhealed'), I jumped to the conclusion that God the Son must have taken *fallen* nature, otherwise the 'every respect' would be a bit of an exaggeration. My underlying soteriology was simple: because fallenness is the problem to be solved, it needs to be part of the solution we confess. Thus I imagined God entering fully into solidarity with us, meeting us in the pigsty, so to speak, suffering and susceptible to death, heading the wrong way in order to heal the prodigal creation.[8] And yet: the theological handbrake had to be applied quite quickly. I was being way too simplistic, as the letter to the

---

7 Hebrews 2:17–18, NRSV, emphasis added.
8 This summary is, of course, influenced by my reading of Karl Barth, *Church Dogmatics*, IV.2

Hebrews made clear. Jesus was 'in every respect ... tested as we are, yet without sin'.[9]

Here, the 'every respect' is heavily qualified. Jesus is *not* like the rest of us because he is without sin. Again, the soteriology is important. The Christian God is not a God who simply shares our condition. The gospel is the story of a God who overcomes our condition through Jesus Christ in his difference as the sinless One in our stead. Thus, the author of Hebrews – having helpfully followed the logic of Christological sameness – sets this second logic in tense parallel. We can call it the saving logic of Christological difference. And, without fear of contradiction, this second logic is applied to the same subject as the first, Jesus of Nazareth.

But how can Jesus be *not* like the rest of us in one respect yet *like* the rest of us in every respect? Something has to give, surely? Or can both logics be run in parallel in a meaningful way? Some historic voices at King's – shaped by their reading of John Owen and Edward Irving – tried to explain how Hebrews' dual logic makes sense if Jesus was fallen *and* without sin.[10] If this was the case, Jesus would share our fallen nature (being really like us) and yet live sinlessly within it. Yet, according to the vast majority of the Christian tradition, any suggestion that Jesus is fallen and without sin is inherently muddled.[11]

---

9 Hebrews 4:15.

10 See again, for example, Alan Spence, 'Christ's Humanity and Ours: John Owen' and Graham W. P. McFarlane, *Christ and Spirit: The Doctrine of the Incarnation according to Edward Irving* (Carlisle: Paternoster Press, 1996). For a helpful mapping of the dogmatic issues in the debate, see the work of former King's student, Kelly M. Kapic, 'The Son's Assumption of a Human Nature: A Call for Clarity', *International Journal of Systematic Theology* 3 (2001), pp. 154–166.

11 For a good summary of the mainstream tradition, see Ian McFarland, 'Fallen or Unfallen? Christ's Human Nature and the Ontology of Human Sinfulness,' *International Journal of Systematic Theology* 10 (October 2008), pp. 401–405. Note also: the debate at King's was never one-sided; see, for example, the work of Oliver Crisp, 'Did Christ have a Fallen Human Nature' in *International Journal of Systematic Theology* 6 (2004), pp. 270–288. Crisp attempts to unpick the logic of the doctrine analytically.

Their logic is simple. If fallenness is a symptom of sin, then it is impossible to be sinless in a fallen nature because this is to have the effect without the cause, a docetic symptom.[12] As a result, with an unbreakable link between sin and fallenness entrenched, the riddle of Hebrews is traditionally explained differently. Fallenness damages our nature from the 'outside', as it were, in no way being *intrinsic* to humanity.[13] Therefore fallenness does not define nature per se, and a fallen nature need not be assumed in order for a nature to be taken because a nature remains nature, damaged or not.[14] Thus, for the mainstream tradition, Christ takes a 'showroom' version of something which the rest of us experience damaged – yet it is *really* a human nature that he takes (even if it is not as we know it!).[15]

However, despite the traditional account explaining Hebrews' dual logic, my troubling questions remained. As I understood it, the majority explanation would imply that the Son of God did somehow have it easier than me, driving a better model of car, so to speak, instead of driving better the damaged model that I inherited. Unhappy with how this conclusion appears to abstract Christ from the reality of my daily struggle, the minority view (that Christ assumed a fallen nature) seemed well worth a second look. To that end, the recent work of Ian McFarland – an American systematic theologian from outside the King's community – proved to be of great help.

Writing in the *International Journal of Systematic Theology*, McFarland demonstrates how the Son can assume a fallen nature *and* remain without sin. McFarland's argument pivots on an important distinction: sin has to do with a *person*; fallenness

---

12 Ian McFarland, 'Fallen or Unfallen?', pp. 401–408.
13 Ian McFarland, 'Fallen or Unfallen?', pp. 405–409.
14 Ian McFarland, 'Fallen or Unfallen?', p. 406.
15 And so – to explain the delivery of Christ's particular undamaged nature – Mary becomes immaculate and sin becomes congenital.

has to do with *nature* – or, in the colloquial terms he employs, sin has to do with the '*who*-ness' of living out '*what*' we are.[16] In other words, McFarland maintains that sin is tied up with the personal agency we live out in the reality we find ourselves in (which is our fallen nature). And, for McFarland, the 'hinge' between the two, so to speak, is the human will which functions as the malleable 'arena' of our nature where our personhood is expressed. He writes:

> *[A] human being is someone rather than something, and thus not adequately or fully described in terms of what they are … The will is the feature of my nature that, as the place where my status as agent is revealed, discloses a limit to my ability to account for my being solely in terms of my whatness.*[17]

In effect, the will – the place *we* are seen – is the indeterminate aspect of our nature which can be shaped with God or against God, *personally*. We all go with the latter. Christ however – the second Person of the Trinity in hypostatic union – lives personally with God through his nature by being wilfully obedient to the Father in fallen humanity. But how is the second Person able to do this? It is here that we return to Gunton's original nudge: the answer has us to do with the work of the Spirit in the triune economy.

As Graham McFarlane – a King's alumnus – has argued, Jesus is the one upon whom the purposes of God are centred intensely.[18] Jesus is the Messiah, the Christ, the anointed One, the one who is set apart by the Spirit from the moment of his

---

16 Ian McFarland, 'Fallen or Unfallen?', pp. 409–412.
17 Ian McFarland, 'Fallen or Unfallen?', pp. 410–411.
18 Graham McFarlane, *Why Do You Believe What You Believe About the Holy Spirit?* (Carlisle: Paternoster Press, 1998).

conception to be the true Israelite who completes everything that Israel anticipated of God. This means that Jesus is 'the epicentre' of the Spirit's work, the place where the Spirit is fully focused and active. Consider, for example, how the Spirit works with Mary, ensuring that Jesus is the product of *God's* creative will, and then how Simeon is enabled by the same Spirit to see the child of promise at his circumcision. Note also the way Jesus is publicly identified and set apart from others at his baptism by the Spirit, before being driven into the desert by the same Spirit, where he overcomes temptations and returns to his mission full of the Spirit. Consider further his self-declaration at the outset of his ministry: 'The Spirit of the Lord is upon me to ...' And the evidential list could go on.[19] As McFarlane sees it, the combined biblical witness is crystal clear: the Spirit sets Jesus apart for God's purpose throughout his life, enabling Jesus to live perfectly before his Father.

And so it was with this pneumatology harnessed to the minority Christology that I began to see – as Gunton encouraged everyone to see – that Irenaeus may have got it right in his struggle against the Gnostic heresies. The Son and the Spirit are best understood as the 'two hands of the Father'.[20] The Son mysteriously cleaves

---

19 Ralph Del Colle sums up helpfully: 'Both the origin and unfolding of Jesus' sonship is pneumatologically grounded, extending from conception (Luke 1:34–35) to messianic inauguration into public ministry (Luke 3:21–23) and culminating in redemptive death (Hebrews 9:14), resurrection (Romans 1:4) and exaltation (John 15:26).' Ralph Del Colle, 'The Triune God' in Colin E. Gunton (ed.), *The Cambridge Companion to Christian Doctrine* (Cambridge: Cambridge University Press, 1997), p. 126.

20 'God needs none of them [i.e. intermediate beings] to do what he predetermined in himself to do, as if he had not his hands. For always there are for him the Word and Wisdom, the Son and Spirit, by whom and in whom he freely and spontaneously does all.' Irenaeus, *Against Heresies* (4.20.1), cited in Colin E. Gunton, *The Triune Creator: A Historical and Systematic Study* (Grand Rapids and Cambridge: Eerdmans, 1998), p. 54 and passim. Gunton's view of Irenaeus is similar to that of Douglas Farrow. Farrow calls Irenaeus a 'prototypical catholic theologian' ('an interpreter of the faith for his own troubled times who bequeathed to subsequent generations of Christians (eastern and western) a great store of theological resources, if not the discipline of church dogmatics per se'). Douglas Farrow, 'St Irenaeus of Lyons – The Church and the World', *Pro Ecclesia 4* (1995) p. 334. Gunton has argued that the metaphor of the 'two

to our fallen humanity, becoming one in hypostatic union with us, possessing a really human nature alongside the creature and before the Father. The second hand, the Spirit, at the same time, is the one within the triune economy who frees the Person of the Son to be fully himself through his human will in union with his Father; or – to use different language – the Spirit perfects the incarnate Son in loving relation to his Father, hovering over the darkness of the deep, creating the second Adam in concert with the Son.

If this account is right, this would suggest that God the Son does not do something *to* us – as an agent working *on* his different pristine humanity, so to speak – but instead graciously does something *with* us in our shared humanity through the enabling economy of the Spirit who works upon him in obedience to the Father.

As a result, with both hands in position, I could see how the Son takes our damaged nature, destined towards death, and is born into this corrupted mess of relations outside Eden. In effect, his nature becomes the primary arena in which the battle takes place.[21] Gloriously victorious in his flesh, Jesus begins the process of re-relating the creation to the Father through the Spirit who enables the reshaping of our damaged humanity through the humanity of the Son. To return to the earlier motorised metaphor: this is a two-handed, panel-beating model of salvation; our nature perfected through the Son's lifelong obedience in the Spirit!

---

hands' is more sophisticated than it may at first appear because our hands are ourselves in action. Colin E. Gunton, *The Promise of Trinitarian Theology*, 2nd edition (London and New York: T&T Clark, 2003), p. 181. Gunton has also detailed the importance and sophistication of metaphor in any theological project. Colin E. Gunton, *The Actuality of Atonement: A Study of Metaphor, Rationality and the Christian Tradition* (London and New York: T&T Clark, 1988), pp. 27–52.

21 Gunton makes the point in conversation with the work of Edward Irving. Colin E. Gunton, *Theology Through the Theologians,* p. 160.

Whatever its merits or defects – and, in theology, we usually find a mixture of both – the foregoing account does have a loud anti-docetic and anti-Apollinarian ring to it, as Gunton himself recognised.[22] Jesus' sufferings and temptations – witnessed to by Scripture – are not pretend or illusory. Not only that, it is not some immanent divine force which kept him from sinning through the course of his life – some sort of autopilot – but instead the work of the Spirit who enables him to live faithfully and freely before the Father as human. This therefore is *recapitulation*. And recapitulation can be understood as some sort of undoing of the ontological damage we've done to ourselves in a way in which the fullness of humanity is established for the first time.[23] Jesus *is* genuinely a second Adam, the One who, through his obedient human will, is perfected by the Spirit through the course of his life as he retraces the desolate steps of the creature before God, unravelling the mess we're in, and *thereby* raising us to the stature of full humanity which Adam never reached. In other words, Jesus becomes *really* human – as in, like us, falling away into nothingness – yet his constant faithfulness reverses the direction, with this particular human blossoming and living a more fully human life than we could ever have imagined – a really, *really* human life, so to speak!

And, if this is the case, all the things that Jesus did – miracles, healings, and the like – the things which we might think prove his divinity could actually reveal his really human humanity – our humanity, transformed from its fallen state through pneumatological obedience. The rest of us still remain in our infancy, with our perfected humanity an eschatological reality, now in some way *sub*-human, but enabled to grow into the

---

22 Colin E. Gunton, *Theology Through the Theologians*, p. 158.
23 For an examination of the doctrine of recapitulation as a reversal that takes us forward, see Douglas Farrow, 'St Irenaeus of Lyons: The Church and World', *Pro Ecclesia* 4 (1995), pp. 333–355.

fullness of Christ by the perfecting work of the same Spirit who – we trust – will enable us to reach our full humanity eschatologically because of the One who was without sin and offered himself on our behalf.

The church is therefore best understood as the great eschatological community of the Spirit, living ahead of time as a great 'experiment', where Christians are called to become fully alive, growing into our redeemed nature, reshaped from our fallenness by the same Spirit in concert with Christ. And for that reason, Jesus – though fully divine – remains of earthly use today because the Spirit who was with him is here with us. Jesus can be a really real example of human life on earth transformed by the work of the Spirit of God.

Of course, on this, much more needs to be said than can be said here, with this chapter being purely an attempt to share a single aspect of the theological conversation taking place at King's under Gunton's supervision. And though the debate concerning the humanity of Christ will no doubt continue, to my mind, Gunton's original nudge deserves applause: a full account of the Spirit's work will run in tandem with a clear account of the mystery of the Son's genuine humanity in the triune economy.

7 DISCERNMENT: THE KEY TO SHARING IN THE MISSION OF GOD

GRAHAM CRAY

In 1963 Lesslie Newbigin wrote: 'It may seem that in stressing the role of the Holy Spirit in the mission of the Church I am simply repeating what everyone knows. And yet I have become convinced that, even when this belief is present and vivid, there are factors in the structures and traditions of our work, which can prevent the belief from becoming effective.'[1] It is a quotation with a surprisingly contemporary ring and relevance.

This chapter is written from the conviction, not only that the work of the Spirit is central and fundamental for Christian mission, but that the task of discerning the activity and leading of the Spirit is the central theological and practical task of a missionary church. The Spirit is the Spirit of Christ. In the book of Revelation the cry of the glorified Lord is that we should 'Listen to what the Spirit is saying to the churches.' 'That cry of Jesus to the church to listen, echoing the Old Testament cry "Hear O Israel", constitutes the church as a school of the

---

1 Lesslie Newbigin, *Trinitarian Doctrine for Today's Mission* (1963), reprinted by Paternoster, 1998, p. 74.

wisdom of Christ, alert to his words and his own embodiment of them.'[2]

Discernment is essential because 'The Holy Spirit is present and active everywhere, but not every development is the work of the Holy Spirit.'[3] Much of what follows comes as a result of rereading John V. Taylor's *The Go-Between God* for the first time in many years. This chapter is in part a conversation with Taylor and in part thoughts triggered by reading Taylor. He wrote that 'We must relinquish our missionary presuppositions and begin in the beginning with the Holy Spirit. This means humbly watching in any situation in which we find ourselves, in order to learn what God is trying to do there, and then doing it with him.'[4] This was not political correctness seeking a moratorium on mission in a multi-faith context. (All New Testament mission is in a multi-faith context!) It is a humble dependence on God and a desire for discernment in each context. Humility is an appropriate word for Christian mission. It implies a proper dependence on God in each situation and a continuing commitment to learn rather than rely on previous experience.[5]

The rediscovery of mission as 'seeing what God is doing and joining in' as Taylor is often paraphrased, is itself based on another rediscovery: the widespread ecumenical rediscovery of the significance of Trinitarian theology and in particular, beginning with Karl Barth, of mission as *Missio Dei* – the mission of God. According to Jürgen Moltmann, 'It is not the

2   David F. Ford, *Christian Worship: Desiring God and Learning in Love* (Cambridge: Cambridge University Press, 2007), p. 254.
3   Kirsteen Kim, *Joining in with the Spirit: Connecting World Church and Local Mission* (Peterborough: Epworth, 2009), p. 35.
4   John V. Taylor, *The Go-Between God: The Holy Spirit and the Christian Mission* (London: SCM Press, 1972), p. 39.
5   For example see *Mission in Bold Humility: David Bosch's Work Considered*, David Jacobus Bosch, Klippies Kritzinger, Willem Saayman, J. J. Kritzinger (eds) (New York: Orbis, 1997), and Tim Chester (ed.), *Justice, Mercy and Humility: Integral Mission and the Poor* (Carlisle: Paternoster, 2002).

Church that has a mission of salvation to fulfil in the world; it is the mission of the Son and the Spirit through the Father that includes the Church.'[6] 'The sending of mission is essentially the sending of the Spirit (John 14:26),' wrote the Orthodox theologian Ion Bria.[7] And Pope John Paul II stated that the Holy Spirit is 'the principle agent of mission'.[8] Put more simply, 'The Church of God does not have a mission, but the God of mission has a Church.'[9]

Things put simply can be misleading. The church has a mission but that mission is participatory in the divine mission, properly understood in Trinitarian terms. 'The mission of the Church is the gift of participating, through the Holy Spirit, in the Son's mission from the Father to the world.'[10] In the New Testament this finds its clearest expression in John 20:21–22: 'As the Father has sent me, so I send you … Receive the Holy Spirit.' Here the Son's work continues – the present continuous tense meaning 'the Father has sent and continues to send me'. The cross and resurrection are 'the end of the beginning' of Christ's work. Now a redeemed church can participate in the work that continues. The Father's sending now includes those who abide in his Son. This is made possible by the work of the Spirit, who leads a Christocentric mission.

This insight simultaneously decreases and increases the church's responsibility for mission. It decreases it because mission is not so much a task to be accomplished as an identity to be fulfilled, and a relationship with God to be enjoyed. 'Mission

---

6 Jürgen Moltmann, *The Church in the Power of the Spirit* (London: SCM Press, 1977), p. 64.
7 Ion Bria, *Go Forth in Peace* (Geneva: WCC, 1986), p. 3.
8 John Paul II 'Redemptoris Missio' Vatican, 1990.
9 Tim Dearborn, *Beyond Duty: A Passion for Christ, a Heart for Mission*, MARC, 1998, quoted in *Mission-Shaped Church*.(London: Church House Publishing, 2004)
10 James Torrance, *Worship, Community and the Triune God of Grace* (Carlisle: Paternoster, 1996), p. ix.

is a Spirit event – it is God's mission, not ours. It is not a duty following the work of Christ but is itself God's work.'[11] The sense of responsibility increases just because it relocates mission from being a task of some in the church to an element (together with worship) of the essence of the church. Mission is part of who we are in God. Andrew Kirk has even suggested that:

> *Mission is so much at the heart of the Church's life, that rather than think of it as one aspect of its existence, it is better to think of it as defining its essence. The Church is by nature missionary to the extent that, if it ceases to be missionary, it has not just failed in one of its tasks, it has ceased being Church.*[12]

It is better to say that a church that does not participate in mission is suffering from amnesia. It has forgotten who it is. In particular, whenever the church finds itself in or called to a new context, it has to rediscover the shape of its missionary engagement. 'The church *is* "missionary by its very nature" and it *becomes* missionary by attending to each and every context in which it finds itself.'[13] This requires discernment and attention to the voice and action of the Spirit.

THE CHARACTERISTICS OF THE SPIRIT'S MINISTRY

Pious intentions to attend to the Spirit can prove to be no more than pious intentions, unless careful attention is paid to the shape and characteristics of the Spirit's ministry. Discernment is blind if it does not know what to look for.

---

11 Clark Pinnock, *Flame of Love* (IVP: Downers Grove, 1996) p. 142.
12 Andrew Kirk, *What is Mission?* (DLT, 1999), p. 30.
13 Stephen B. Bevans and Roger P. Schroeder, *Constants in Context* (New York: Orbis 2004), p. 2.

Taylor provides the essential perspective. 'Our theology would improve if we thought more of the church being given to the Spirit than of the Spirit being given to the church.'[14] Mission is participation in the continuing ministry of Christ, made actual through the presence of the Holy Spirit. The church has been given to the Spirit, and the Spirit to the church, for this purpose.

The characteristics of the Holy Spirit's ministry are set out under the following headings:

The leader of mission
The Go-Between God opens with this statement:

> *The chief actor in the historic mission of the Christian church is the Holy Spirit. He is the director of the whole enterprise. The mission consists of the things that he is doing in the world. In a special way it consists of the light that he is focussing upon Jesus Christ.*[15]

The Spirit does not merely empower the church's mission, although that is essential. Nor does the Spirit direct that mission, as though from a distance, from 'head office'. The Spirit is the leading missionary, both ahead and in charge as the chief practitioner. Commentating on John 15, and then 16, Lesslie Newbigin wrote 'It is not said that the Spirit will help the disciple to bear witness .... What is said is that the Spirit will bear witness and that – secondarily – the disciples are witnesses.'[16] And 'He is the powerful advocate who goes before

---

14 John V. Taylor, *op. cit.*, p. 133.
15 John V. Taylor, *op. cit.*, p. 3.
16 Lesslie Newbigin, *The Light Has Come* (Grand Rapids, MI: Eerdmans, 1982), p. 216.

the church to bring the world under conviction.'[17] Discernment requires 'seeing what God is doing and joining in' because, as the story of Peter and Cornelius demonstrates, 'God is already ahead of all evangelism, carrying on his mission to the world .... More often than not respectful discernment will demand drastic changes of heart and mind, as for Peter with his own traditions.'[18] Without the action of God, not just empowerment from God, there is no mission, even if a great deal of human energy is expended. 'The shape of empowered mission is not arrived at ideologically, or even pragmatically. In mission we ask not just "Is this action good and necessary?" We also ask, "Where is God leading? Is this God's undertaking?"... Spirit leadership is central.'[19]

Reliable and unpredictable

The New Testament describes the Spirit as both a stable, reliable presence in the believer and the church and as an unpredictable actor who continually takes the church unawares. There is both supreme safety and continual risk in life in the Spirit. Taylor describes the Spirit as: 'Not exceptional endowment but permanent presence, not so much of a power but a partner.'[20] But, with strong echoes in the book of Acts, he also says, 'Mission is often described as if it were a planned extension of an old building. But in fact it has usually been more like an unexpected explosion.'[21]

This creative tension between stable indwelling presence, assuring us that in Christ we are adopted children of God, and obedience to the Spirit as the leader of Christ's mission can be

---

17 Lesslie Newbigin, *op. cit.*, p. 211.
18 David Ford and Daniel Hardy, *Knowing and Praising God* (Philadelphia: Westminster, 1985), p. 151.
19 Clark Pinnock, p. 145.
20 John V. Taylor, p. 84f.
21 John V. Taylor p,. 53.

seen in the life and writing of Paul.[22] Equally, in John's Gospel the new advocate comes to be with the disciples for ever and yet those born of the Spirit are like the wind which 'blows where it chooses, and you hear the sound of it, but you do not know where it comes from or where it goes'. This assuring yet elusive role of the Spirit has been described as a gift, not a possession. 'The Holy Spirit is quintessentially a gift of God, and one that is not simply possessed when given, rather the mark of having received it is to ask for it continually, so that the all pervasive and constitutive cry of the church is "Come, Holy Spirit".'[23]

Relational

Taylor's key insight was to understand the fundamentally relational nature of the Spirit's ministry. Treating each phrase of 'the grace' in 2 Corinthians 13:13 as an indication of the essence of the ministry of each divine person – the love of God the Father and the grace of the Lord Jesus Christ – Taylor saw the essential ministry of the Spirit as creating and forming relationship. He wrote of 'the in-between-ness of the Holy Spirit', of 'this invisible go-between' and thus of 'The Go-Between God'. Taylor recognised the fundamentally corporate nature of life in the Spirit. 'Only in their togetherness can Christians remain alight with the fire of the Spirit.'[24]

This raises the question of whether discernment might be a fundamentally corporate faculty, although also exercised by individuals. This was the conclusion of James Dunn from his study of the relevant Pauline texts. 'It is almost impossible to avoid the exegetical conclusion that the gift of discernment is the prerogative of all – not to be exercised by just a few,

---

22 For example Romans 8 and Romans 15.
23 David Ford, p. 261.
24 John V. Taylor. p. 133.

but to be exercised by the whole community.'[25] At the heart of discernment is the capacity to recognise interconnectedness. Both in each missional context, and within our selves, what are the patterns that help us understand the Spirit's activity? 'No wonder the disciples must wait for the promise of the Spirit. For it is he alone, working in the deepest recesses of our being, who arranges the meaningless pieces of reality until they suddenly fall into shape.'[26]

Anticipates the future in the present

The New Testament's teaching about the Spirit has a distinctive shape to it. The Spirit is the present anticipation of the future Christ has secured. As a New Testament scholar, Gordon Fee, summarises this: 'the Spirit is "the *certain evidence* that the future had dawned, and the *absolute guarantee"* of its final consummation.'[27] Colin Gunton made the same point as a doctrine scholar: 'The action of the Spirit is to anticipate, in the present and by means of the finite and contingent, the things of the age to come.'[28]

The importance of this for discernment can clearly be seen in Peter's speech on the day of Pentecost. He claims that the outpouring of the Spirit is the direct fulfilment of the prophecy of Joel. 'In the last days, God says, I will pour out my Spirit on all people. Your sons and daughters will prophesy, your young men will see visions, your old men will dream dreams. Even on my servants, both men and women, I will pour out my Spirit in those days, and they will prophesy[NIV].'[29] Peter distinguishes between the 'last days' which have begun with this outpouring,

25 James Dunn, *The Christ and the Spirit*, Vol. 2 (T&T Clark, 1998), p. 321.
26 John V. Taylor, p. 70.
27 Gordon Fee, *God's Empowering Presence* (Peabody: Hendrickson, 1994), p. 806.
28 Colin Gunton, *The Promise of Trinitarian Theology* (Edinburgh: T &T Clark, 1991), p. 68.
29 Acts 2:17-18.

and 'the Lord's great and glorious day' (verse 20). In this in – between time the gift of the Spirit is now given to all God's children, irrespective of age, gender or social status. And the Spirit is given, no longer just to prophets, priests and kings, or temporarily for a specific cause. The Spirit is given in this way to guide the church. Prophecies, dreams and visions may now come through all for all. It is the mission of the Holy Spirit to guide the church to be an imperfect foretaste of the future Christ has secured, specific to its own time and culture.

Presses on to completion

There is a holy impatience about the Holy Spirit. The Spirit presses on to the final completion of God's work through Christ. Where patience is required that fruit of the Spirit is developed, but the Spirit also empowers us to persist until the end. The taste we receive of the future kingdom becomes a compass that gives direction to the remainder of our lives. 'By the Spirit's presence believers tasted of the life to come and became oriented towards its consummation.'[30] 'The presence of the Holy Spirit ... stirs up the desire and yearning for the coming kingdom and the full rule of the king. The Spirit of God is always pushing towards the completion of all things.'[31]

The Spirit of Christ

If the Spirit stirs up a desire for the coming kingdom, it is because the kingdom is 'the kingdom of our God and of his Christ'. The Spirit is above all the Spirit of Christ. And making Christ known lies at the heart of Christian mission. 'Christians ... are caught up into the desire of the Spirit of God to make men profoundly aware of Jesus Christ, of what he is himself, and of what he

---

30 Gordon Fee, *op. cit.*, p. 810.
31 Peter Hocken, *The Holy Spirit & the Coming Kingdom*, Skepsis (in *Anglican Renewal Ministries* magazine).

makes available to the whole world, so that in him they may be confronted by the question and the call of God, and make their free choice.'[32] To know Christ is also to be caught up in the Father's purposes through Christ. This involves an abandoning of our separate agendas and a discovering of ourselves and our true purpose in him. This may seem profoundly risky but could not be more safe. As Taylor says, 'If the Spirit is making Jesus more real, neither caution nor convention, nor reputation nor love for any other creature ought to make us resist his possession of us.'[33]

But the reality that the Spirit is the Spirit of Christ has another connection with mission and discernment. The church is the body of Christ, the fullness of him who fills everything. Christ takes shape in human communities called the church in each era and culture. As Eugene Peterson says, he 'plays in ten thousand places'. There is both a givenness about the church which makes it authentic and identifiable in each place, but there is also a specificity for each contest. Zizoulos contrasts these as the institution and the constitution of the church, relating one to Christ and the other to the Spirit. 'Christ in-stitutes (the Church) and the Spirit con-stitutes.' 'The "in-stitution" is something presented to us, more or less a fait-accompli... The "con-stitution" is something that involves us in its very being, something that we accept freely because we take part in its very emergence.'[34] Rowan Williams and David F. Ford have made similar points about the role of the Spirit in shaping the church. 'The Son is manifest in a single, paradigmatic, figure. The Spirit is manifest in the "translatability" of that into the contingent diversity of history.'[35] 'It is as if the Spirit of Christ allows his

---

32 John V. Taylor, p. 136.
33 John V. Taylor, p. 62.
34 John Zizoulos, *Being As Communion* (New York: SVS Press, 1985), p. 130.
35 Rowan Williams, *On Christian Theology* (Oxford: Blackwell Publishers, 2000), p.

imitator to become multiply incarnate by identifying with many types of people, very different among themselves.'[36]

It is the role of the Spirit to guide the church about its shape with each culture and context; helping it to evade both irrelevance and syncretism. It is the calling of the church to discern the wisdom of the Spirit.

THE NATURE AND PRACTICE OF DISCERNMENT

If these factors exemplify the Spirit's ministry, they must also aid the practice of discernment. Mission is blind without discernment. Taylor wrote that 'The main concerns of any missionary training ... should be to help people to become more receptive to the revelation of God.'[37] He saw the imbalance of Western forms of knowledge in that 'We have greatly extended our power to transmit, to communicate ... but not our power to receive.'[38]

If the work of the Spirit has distinctive characteristics, so also has discernment. I will identify six in all, but they should be regarded like the ingredients of a recipe. Just as it is the blending together of ingredients in the right way that leads to culinary success, so discernment within mission depends on the integration of these characteristics, and suffers when one is missing – like forgetting the salt.

Douglas McBain, author of one of the few books on discernment to be written from within the UK charismatic movement, identifies the first two ingredients. 'Discernment is mature grace. It combines the capacity to pick up unseen spiritual signals with the ability to rightly interpret them. It is a unique

---

125f.
36 David F. Ford, p. 188.
37 John V. Taylor, p. 70.
38 John V. Taylor, p. 65.

quality in which charism and character combine.'[39] Discernment requires the appropriate *charism*. It is located within the range of the gifts of the Holy Spirit. This is encouraging. Many of the charismata identified in the New Testament are in this sense revelatory. There is a 'gift of distinguishing between spirits', there are words of wisdom and knowledge, and a range of prophetic gifts. Furthermore the gifts of the Spirit are contextual rather than allocated. It is perfectly true that over time many Christians develop a mature ministry in a particular area of the charismata, that the ministry of each is for the whole and that each needs the ministry of the others. Discernment is normally communal. But underlying this is also the basic reality that the gifts are the tools for the tasks to which the Spirit has called us. In each context we can trust God for the gifts we need, rather than be stuck because we 'have healing' and we need 'prophecy'. Discernment is possible because the Spirit has us, not because we happen to have the right gifts. McBain sees this all as a matter of grace. God is not like Pharaoh. He does not say 'Make bricks and find your own straw!' We can trust God to provide the gifts needed for discernment. But we need the Spirit's gifts and not just the sum of our own previous experience.

But McBain also connects discernment to *character*, to maturity. In the New Testament the charismata are not evidence of maturity. The Corinthian church was not lacking any of them, but was castigated for its immaturity. The youngest Christian can exercise spiritual gifts, but discernment normally requires stability of character. McBain writes 'No spiritual gift has value if divorced from love, gentleness and self-control. Discernment totally ceases to operate in their absence.'[40]

Where there is no maturity the church is vulnerable to being

---

39 Douglas McBain, *Discerning the Spirits* (Basingstoke: Marshall Pickering, 1992), p. 198.
40 Douglas McBain, p. 198.

'blown by any wind of ...' There is a direct connection between maturity and consistent discernment.

Walter Moberly's study on 'human speech on behalf of God' in the Bible confirms the necessity of character and identifies a further ingredient.[41] Moberley sees 'Two prime criteria of discernment: on the one hand, disposition, character and lifestyle, on the other hand, a message whose content and searching challenge reflect God's priorities and seek to engender unreserved engagement with God.'[42] *Content* is the third ingredient: a content that draws us deeper into God's purposes rather than telling us what we want to hear. This is to counter our tendency to filter the Bible and our listening to the Spirit through the grid of our convenience and our comfort zones. It also relates discernment closely to our being drawn more fully into the purposes of God.

Next we need to add the *characteristics* of the Spirit's ministry, which we have identified in the first part of this paper. When we are trying to discern if something is a Spirit-shaped development, we can treat the question as one of a worldview. To what extent are our expectations shaped by the characteristic work of the Spirit, and to what extent has another less adequate worldview or mindset misdirected our thinking or seeing? For example, a dualistic worldview which saw everything as the direct action of the Spirit or the devil, each within their own sphere, has no capacity to 'see what God is doing' in the world, as it does not believe he is there.

We saw earlier that the relational nature of the Spirit's ministry makes discernment a fundamentally corporate or *communal* activity. At certain times Christians may expect personal guidance. The Spirit addresses individuals at various places in Acts. But major developments – in particular the extension of

---

41 Walter Moberly, *Prophecy and Discernment* (Cambridge: CUP, 2006), p.1
42 *Op. cit*, pp. 232f.

the gospel to the Gentiles – required corporate confirmation. In the local church, claims to speak for the Spirit need to be weighed in the assembly.

If discernment has this corporate quality it makes particular demands upon leaders.[43] They may not see themselves as the ones through whom God speaks. Their role is to facilitate the church as it listens to God together. It is a cultivating role. 'Leadership is about cultivating an environment that innovates and releases the missional imagination present in a community of God's people ... An environment in which the Spirit-given presence of God's future may emerge among the people of God.'[44] If the Spirit of God is present then it is possible for a congregation to identify the ways in which it is called to live as an imperfect local foretaste of the future Christ has secured. It is the work of the Spirit to guide this process of discernment, and to empower the church to live accordingly. It is the role of leaders to help people to listen to the Spirit and to oversee the process. 'Leadership is about connecting, not controlling. It is about bringing people together for the purpose of creative synergy.'[45]

Discernment has a recipe that comprises charism, character, content, characteristics, community and cultivating leadership. It is the church's key to sharing in the mission of God. But it is never sufficient to have a recipe and the right ingredients – unless you have no interest in eating. The church in our changed and rapidly changing context needs to learn again the art of discernment.

Let anyone who has an ear listen to what the Spirit is saying to the churches.[46]

---

43 I have applied this material directly to the practice of leadership in Graham Cray 'Discerning Leadership', Grove Leadership 1.
44 Alan Roxburgh and Fred Romanuk, *The Missional Leader* (San Francisco: Jossey-Bass, 2006) pp. 5, 9.
45 Eddie Gibbs, *Leadership Next* (Leicester: IVP, 2005) p. 93.
46 Revelation 2:7, 11, 17, 29; 3:6, 13, 22.

8 THE SPIRIT AND THE CROSS: ENGAGING A KEY CRITIQUE OF CHARISMATIC PNEUMATOLOGY

SIMEON ZAHL

In the century since the revival events at Azusa Street in Los Angeles in 1906, the global proliferation of Pentecostal and charismatic expressions of Christianity has been nothing short of extraordinary. As Allan Anderson puts it, it would appear that 'in less than a century, Pentecostal, Charismatic, and associated movements have become the largest numerical force in world Christianity after the Roman Catholic Church and represent a quarter of all Christians'.[1] It is only in recent decades that scholars of Christianity have begun to take these developments as seriously as they deserve, however. One immediate difficulty has been that of definition: what, exactly, is 'Pentecostalism'? What features characterise 'charismatic' theology and practice? Does having a 'charismatic' view of the Holy Spirit's activity in the world today necessarily make you a 'Pentecostal'? This question of what is distinctive in these movements has, more than any other, shaped recent academic discussion among Pentecostal and charismatic theologians.

---

1   Allan Anderson, *An Introduction to Pentecostalism: Global Charismatic Christianity* (Cambridge: Cambridge University Press, 2004), p. 1.

It is widely agreed at this point that the common judgement earlier in the twentieth century, that *glossolalia* – speaking in tongues – is the primary distinguishing feature, is a superficial one, as it recognises neither the abiding disagreements among Pentecostals, both early on and more recently, on this issue, nor the theological complexity of Pentecostalism's matrix of premillenial eschatology, miraculous healing, and Wesleyan Holiness theology, to name just three of the most salient elements. Perhaps the single most significant distinctive for both charismatics and Pentecostals, though by no means the only such distinctive, is a type of personal charismatic experience of the Spirit, particularly among those who are already believers. Allan Anderson makes the point well:

> *all the various expressions of Pentecostalism have one common experience, that is a personal encounter with the Spirit of God enabling and empowering people for service ... Through their experience of the Spirit, Pentecostals and Charismatics make the immanence of God tangible ... Although different Pentecostals and Charismatics do not always agree on the precise formulation of their theology of the Spirit, the emphasis on divine encounter and the resulting transformation of life is always there. This is what likens Pentecostals to the mystical traditions, perhaps more than any other contemporary form of Christianity.*[2]

Charismatics of many stripes describe a particular moment or series of moments of being 'filled with the Spirit', by which is usually meant a powerful, intimate, and affectively charged

---

2 Anderson, *Pentecostalism*, pp. 187–188. Macchia makes the similar claim that Spirit baptism understood 'as a post-conversion charismatic experience' is 'the crown jewel of Pentecostal distinctives' (Frank D. Macchia, *Baptized in the Spirit: A Global Pentecostal Theology* (Grand Rapids, MI: Zondervan, 2006), p. 20).

encounter with the Spirit of God. Such encounters often, though not always, take place during a period of prayer or worship. Closely related are several other types of experience, such as a kind of direct communication or leading from God (eg, 'words of knowledge', prophetic dreams, or a certain kind of strong conviction attributed to the Spirit) and miraculous experience such as healing.[3] A church where such experiences are looked for regularly is often characterised as 'Spirit-filled', understood in contrast to non-charismatic churches. Experience of the Spirit of this kind, which makes 'the immanence of God tangible', is enormously compelling, and appears to speak very deeply to the spiritual needs and desires of twentieth-century and now twenty-first-century people. This is true in different ways across the globe and in an astonishing variety of contexts, as the global explosion of charismatic Christianity demonstrates.

With this power, however, come real vulnerabilities. One critique, in particular, has long been lodged against theologies emphasising affectively-charged spiritual experience, and it needs to be taken very seriously by charismatics today: namely, that *such theologies are particularly prone to the problem of spiritual self-deception*. The idea is that people claiming to have experience of the Spirit and the Spirit's guidance can often be self-deceived, and may really be unconsciously 'baptising' their own wishes and desires by attributing them to God.

In what follows, I will examine this critique, and then propose a pneumatological principle that remains robustly charismatic while taking concerns about self-deception very seriously.

---

3 For a typology of different varieties of experience of the Spirit in charismatic and Pietist traditions, see Simeon Zahl, *Pneumatology and Theology of the Cross in the Preaching of Christoph Friedrich Blumhardt: The Holy Spirit between Wittenberg and Azusa Street* (London: T&T Clark/Continuum, 2010), pp. 88–93. Several of the points made in this essay follow or build upon the more extended treatment there.

No theologian has voiced concern about experience-oriented pneumatologies more incisively than Protestant Reformer Martin Luther, and a discussion of his version of the critique is an appropriate place to begin. The way towards a charismatic response to Luther is indicated by the pneumatology of a remarkable figure from the late nineteenth and early twentieth century, Pietist theologian and healer Christoph Friedrich Blumhardt, and the second section will give an account of his approach, which expected the Spirit to act powerfully and unmediatedly in lives and communities, but to do so most reliably in 'negative' experiences of suffering and the thwarting of human egocentrism. In the concluding section, I will build on Blumhardt's thinking to describe certain implications of his approach for our understanding of the Spirit, particularly in terms of its freedom and its creativity.

LUTHER'S CRITIQUE OF CHARISMATIC PNEUMATOLOGIES

In the 1520s, Martin Luther engaged in a series of debates with Andreas von Karlstadt and other members of the 'Radical Reformation' over the activity of the Spirit. Historically, it is anachronistic to call Luther's opponents in these debates 'charismatics'. What we call 'charismatic and Pentecostal Christianity' is a phenomenon that traces its roots to Los Angeles in 1906, nearly 400 years after Luther's writings on the subject. Theologically, however, it is remarkable how much similarity there is between contemporary charismatic pneumatologies and Luther's characterisation of those he called 'enthusiasts' or *Schwärmer*. This is clear not least from that fact that many of his critiques of the 'enthusiasts' prove to be quite prescient when applied to contemporary charismatic theology, particularly in some of its less laudable and more extreme tendencies (like the tendency towards a gospel of 'prosperity' and success, or the proclivity for institutional upheaval and splintering).[4]

The heart of Luther's critique was the problem of self-deception: the accusation that the 'enthusiasts' were claiming to have experienced the Spirit and the Spirit's guidance when really they were just unconsciously taking their own personal wishes and desires and attributing them to God's leading. As he put it rather harshly, 'If you ask who directs them to teach and act in this way, they point upward and reply, "Ah, God tells me so, and the Spirit says so." Indeed, all idle dreams [for them] are nothing but God's Word.'[5] Luther was deeply aware of the ongoing reality of sin in Christians, and so became very nervous when people made claims to have heard directly from God through the Spirit, or through signs, or to have had a remarkable experience of God's Spirit. He thought that people are very quick to try to bring God in to justify their own interests, even if they are not aware they are doing so.

Luther's question is a probing one, and must be taken seriously by charismatic Christians. Its spectre is particularly present in the common pastoral occurrence of when someone feels convinced of God's leading in a certain direction and that 'leading' ends up proving untrue. For example, they might be convinced the Spirit has told them they will get a certain job or marry a particular person, but they do not get the job after all, or the relationship ends abruptly. The 'leading' may just

---

4 For more extended analysis of contemporary charismatic theology in light of Luther's critiques, see Zahl, *Pneumatology and Theology of the Cross,* pp. 178–181. For acknowledgment of some of these tendencies by scholars of the Pentecostal and charismatic movements, see for example, Anderson, *Pentecostalism*, pp. 157–159; and Harvey Cox, *Fire from Heaven: The Rise of Pentecostal Spirituality and the Reshaping of Religion in the Twenty-first Century* (Cambridge, MA: Da Capo Press, 1995), pp. 77–78.

5 Martin Luther, *Against the Heavenly Prophets in the Matter of Images and Sacraments, 1525,* trans. Conrad Bergendorff, and Bernhard Erling, *Luther's Works* Vol. 40 (Philadelphia: Muhlenberg Press, 1958), p. 148.

have been their own desire, subconsciously attributed in some way to God (though there are more complex ways to interpret such events). It is also present in one of the more troubling developments in a number of Pentecostal theologies, that of the so-called 'prosperity gospel', which holds that God's reliable will in people's lives includes granting them health, material prosperity, and financial success. One can see why someone like Luther might say that a person attracted to a 'prosperity' approach just wants health or financial security for their own sake, and that they have brought God in, in an idolatrous way, to baptise or ratify an otherwise quite straightforward – and understandable – human desire.

Luther's theological response to the problem of self-deception in light of the ongoing reality of sin in Christians was to reject what we would now call charismatic pneumatology outright. He argued instead that the Spirit acts reliably, particularly in a saving way, through the preaching of the scriptural word *only*. Biblical preaching and the sacraments of baptism and the Lord's Supper (the latter because they are explicitly sanctioned by the word), are the sole reliable instruments through which the Spirit works. God does act through his Spirit in ways that are experienceable in our inner selves and our feelings, but this activity is always mediated through the external word. As Luther puts it:

> *Now when God sends forth his holy gospel he deals with us in a twofold manner, first outwardly, then inwardly. Outwardly he deals with us through the oral word of the gospel and through material signs, that is, baptism and the sacrament of the altar. Inwardly he deals with us through the Holy Spirit, faith, and other gifts. But whatever their measure or order the outward factors should and must precede. The inward experience follows and is effected by*

116

the outward. God has determined to give the inward to no one except through the outward .... Observe carefully, my brother, this order, for everything depends on it.[6]

The upshot of this is that Luther radically prioritises the Bible over personal experience of the Holy Spirit. The latter only takes place, in his view, as a result of contact with the former.[7] This is the only way, he believes, to preserve Christians from the very great danger of self-deception and of being misled by the devil in spiritual experience and direct divine guidance. The old Reformation slogan, *sola scriptura* (scripture alone), in part means scripture alone *as opposed to most forms of charismatic experience*.

Luther's critique is a powerful and troubling one. However, his antidote to the self-deception problem, for all its merits, is simply too strong. Does God really *never* guide people or interact with them directly outside biblical preaching and the sacraments? Is the Bible not full of stories of people being stopped in their tracks, more or less out of nowhere, by experiences of God? One thinks of Paul on the road to Damascus, or of that wonderfully random verse about Samson receiving the Spirit in his youth: 'The Spirit of the Lord began to stir in [Samson] in Mahaneh-Dan, between Zorah and Eshtaol' (Judges 13:25). Or pastorally, does God not sometimes speak at odd times, and through unexpected means, like a song on the radio, or a novel, or a passing comment in a conversation? What about the remarkable vision Augustine, in his *Confessions*, describes having with his mother Monica shortly before her death, which came about not

---

6 Martin Luther, *Against the Heavenly Prophets*, p. 126.

7 In some places, especially in his earlier writings, Luther expressed a more complex view; the above represents the key point in his mature pneumatology, developed over the course of the debates with the 'enthusiasts' in the 1520s, and codified in particular in *The Smalcald Articles* (Part III, section 8).

through a sermon or through Bible study but simply through a discussion about heaven with a dying woman?[8] And is not one of the defining qualities of the Spirit in the Bible its freedom, its creativity, and its unpredictability? Jesus tells us in John's Gospel that 'The wind [Spirit] blows wherever it pleases. You hear its sound, but you cannot tell where it comes from or where it is going' (John 3:8 NIV). Luther's Spirit, by contrast, seems to blow in the highly predictable pattern of preached word and sacrament. Furthermore, the sheer power of personal experience of the Spirit to transform lives and congregations – witnessed currently on the scale of hundreds of millions of charismatics and Pentecostals worldwide – is an astonishing force to be reckoned with in the early twenty-first century, and the church loses touch with this affective, emotional side of its witness at its peril.

Luther is of course right to give the Bible *priority* in all sorts of ways, and it should always be the premier pastoral and theological touchstone for our experiences of God. But to give it absolute and *exclusive* priority in the way he does is going too far.

If we do not go so far with Luther, however, a new question arises: how are we nevertheless to take very seriously his concerns about human nature and self-deception? Just because not *all* charismatic spiritual experience is tied up with self-deception does not mean that *none* of it ever is! Human beings do remain sinners, to whatever degree, after receiving the Spirit; even the most devout are still what Augustine called 'a vast deep' in their inner selves, often driven by desires and impulses they neither understand nor control;[9] and Christians do not finally move beyond the possibility of deeply misreading the work of the Spirit in their lives and decisions.

---

8 Augustine, *Confessions,* trans. Henry Chadwick (New York: Oxford University Press, 1992), pp. 170–172.
9 Augustine, *Confessions*, p. 66.

THE CRUCIFORM ACTIVITY OF THE SPIRIT

I would like to propose a principle for spiritual discernment that I think needs to be born closely in mind alongside other such principles (like conformity to the witness of Scripture, or John's criteria of the witness of love and Christological orientation[10]). It takes account of some of Luther's concerns without closing the door to charismatic experience. The principle is this:

One of the most reliable ways in which the Spirit acts in our lives is through 'negative', cruciform experiences: through suffering, the thwarting of our egos, and the uncomfortable disruption of usual patterns of relating to the world, to each other, and to God.

We see this sort of activity of the Spirit in John 16:8, where we are told that one of the Spirit's roles is to 'convict the world of sin and righteousness and judgement'. In other words, the Spirit is also the *Holy* Spirit. Likewise, when people are convicted of sin through the law of God, properly speaking such conviction is the activity of the Spirit. Another way of understanding this is to talk about the freedom of the Spirit: often when the Spirit blows where *it* wishes, that means it is not blowing where *we* wish! Sometimes, like with Jonah, the Spirit sends people to Nineveh, very much against their will and even their best efforts to the contrary. It is the Spirit, too, who led Jesus out into the desert to be starved and tempted (Matthew 4:1; Mark 1:12; Luke 4:1–2). When people have so-called 'desert experiences', where God feels painfully silent or distant or absent, they may well be experiencing the Spirit in that very fact. This also means that sometimes a church that looks stagnant or is numerically 'in decline' has not in fact been abandoned by the Spirit – and vice versa. Or to put the principle in the most proper theological perspective: Jesus'

---

10 The latter two are both expressed in 1 John 4.

119

anointed, Spirit-led path, following his baptism by the Spirit, led him on a direct line to crucifixion and death.

Few theologians have understood better *both* the activity of the Spirit in blessings like healing *and* the activity of the Spirit in the 'negative' than Christoph Friedrich Blumhardt (1842–1919). Blumhardt was a Pietist preacher and theologian from southern Germany, and an important figure in the pre-history of the Pentecostal and charismatic movements, known for his gift of supernatural healing prayer. He explains the principle I am describing very well:

> *What we notice when we observe the lives of true apostles and prophets is the pain of childbirth – a struggle for something that does not yet exist, but for the sake of which they are willing to give up everything they have. Although they may find a kind of peace with God in this struggle, **the reliable mark of the Holy Spirit at work is not so much divine peace as birth-pangs, the anxiety and unsettled feeling that accompanies profound change.** Were the pangs to cease and only peace remain, it would soon turn out to be a false peace, like a woman whose birth-pangs cease and her child is stillborn.*[11]

By remembering that very often the Spirit is more reliably present in the things that thwart egos and disrupt human plans and expectations – what Blumhardt, picking up on John 16:4–22 and Romans 8:22–23, calls 'birth-pangs' – it is possible to take Luther's concern about self-deception more seriously than it otherwise would be. We are not as likely to make up or deceive ourselves about difficult and deeply uncomfortable

---

11 Christoph Friedrich Blumhardt, *Damit Gott kommt: 'Gedanken aus dem Reich Gottes'* (Giessen/Basel: Brunnen Verlag, 1992), p. 179, emphasis added..

things as we are about blessings. If the activity of the Spirit in the world is to free us for a fuller, 'Christ-shaped' humanity, as Rowan Williams helpfully asserts,[12] then Blumhardt's approach could be described as emphasising the 'cruciform' component of that shape.

IMPLICATIONS OF THE CROSS-SHAPED SPIRIT

For Christoph Blumhardt, this principle had a number of concrete implications over the course of his life, and each is instructive of the possible meanings of this 'cruciform' approach to the Spirit. Ethically, in Blumhardt's particular late nineteenth- and early twentieth-century German context, it helped confirm his conviction that the rise of Socialism among industrial workers, deeply uncomfortable to middle-class Christians at the time, was actually one of the places God was very likely to be at work in late nineteenth-century German society: challenging the political comfort zone of most German Christians, and doing so on behalf of the marginalised. In one speech from 1900, Blumhardt identifies the poor, meek, and persecuted of the Beatitudes directly with the industrial working class: 'Today you have to say: blessed are the proletariat, for the Kingdom of Heaven is coming to them.'[13] Likewise, Blumhardt's remarkable critique of militaristic nationalism in the First World War, fifteen years later, can be attributed in significant part to his expectation that the Spirit's action in the world most reliably takes the form not of triumphalism or 'us vs. them' thinking, but of the cross.[14]

---

12 See Rowan Williams's discussion in Chapter 4 of this book–specifically, p.68.

13 Christoph Friedrich Blumhardt, *Seid Auferstandene! 1890–1906*, vol. II, Ansprachen, Predigten, Reden, Briefe: 1865–1917 (Neukirchen-Vluyn: Neukirchener Verlag, 1978), p. 217, as reported in the *Schwäbische Tagwacht*.

14 For more on Blumhardt's critical voice during the First World War, see Simeon Zahl, 'Rethinking "Enthusiasm": Christoph Blumhardt on the Discernment of the Spirit',

Pastorally, Blumhardt's 'cruciform' approach to the Spirit helped give him deep insight into tendencies towards pious complacency and legalistic hypocrisy among active and devoted Christians, himself included. Often, as he puts it:

*Piety itself becomes just a zeal for our own well-being, and Sunday services are only meant to help **us**, and prayer[15] is supposed to be a remedy for **us**. Bible, altar, Sunday service, teaching and admonition: all of it is just used in service of our own ends, our own lives, our own activities.*

In this sermon from the 1880s, Blumhardt exhorts his congregation therefore to recognise 'our great guilt for seeking not God but ourselves, even as Christians'.[16] The target here is an egoistic and therefore hypocritical use of Christian practices and beliefs to make oneself feel better in relation to God, or to gain God's favour, or to win the approval of one's Christian peers. For Blumhardt, more often it is in failures of piety – failures to love or to pray or to give God proper priority – and, similarly, in the revelation of sin rather than its removal – the crashing realisation of the subtle, rationalised self-interest behind much Christian practice – that the Spirit is most powerfully and actively present. This is what Blumhardt meant with his remarkable statement, 'I prefer the reality of sin to the swindle of religions.'[17] In his view, God prefers honesty about sin to pious behaviour that attempts to elide over it, and

International Journal of Systematic Theology 12, no. 3 (2010), pp. 356–360.

15 Part of what Blumhardt has in mind here is charismatic healing prayer in particular, as will become clear below.

16 Christoph Friedrich Blumhardt, *Sterbet, so wird Jesus leben! Predigten und Andachten aus den Jahren 1888 bis 1896*, vol. II, Eine Auswahl aus seinen Predigten, Andachten, und Schriften (Erlenbach-Zürich: Rotapfel-Verlag, 1925), pp. 148, 149, emphasis added.

17 Blumhardt, *Seid Auterstandene!*, p. 195.

sometimes the Spirit's role is simply to reveal, uncomfortably, the hypocrisy of such behaviour rather than to make people outwardly 'better' Christians.

Blumhardt's approach to *charismatic* experience of the Spirit, in particular, is evident in a remarkable episode from the 1890s. Like his father, Johann Christoph Blumhardt (1805–1880), Christoph had an international reputation for supernatural healing prayer. For most of his life, he ran a retreat centre in the town of Bad Boll to which people would come from all over Germany, Switzerland and beyond in order to receive prayer from him for specific physical or spiritual ailments. As a result of this healing ministry, the two Blumhardts are considered important figures in the pre-history of the Pentecostal movement.[18]

In the early 1890s, however, Blumhardt became convinced that although the healings were still taking place, God's will was for him to stop performing such prayer for a time. The reason was, in his view, that people had become more interested in being healed than in the God doing the healing. Starting in March 1894, therefore, he publicly refused for a few years to accept any more of what he saw as 'self-seeking' prayer requests. He drew up a stock letter, which was sent to everyone who wrote to him for prayer for healing or some other trouble. In it he outlined his cross-centred approach to the Spirit, and explained why he would no longer pray these sorts of prayers:

It is as if nearly all of [those who write to me] have turned [in their prayers] to a kind of exploitation of God's grace

---

18 See Anderson, Pentecostalism, pp. 24, 30; and Donald W. Dayton, Theological Roots of Pentecostalism (Peabody, MA: Hendrickson Publishers, 1987), pp. 120–121. As a result of this reputation, Blumhardt was invited by William Boardman to a major pre-Azusa Street healing conference that took place in the UK in 1885 (the 'International Conference on Divine Healing and True Holiness'), though he declined the invitation. See Christoph friedrich Blumhardt, *Von der Kirche zum keich Gottes: 1865-1889* (Neukirchener Verlag, 1978), pp. 77-79.

*and compassion. The Saviour becomes merely our personal
servant, whose job is just to fix again and again whatever we
have ruined ... I cannot and may not continue praying for
God to give aid to this person or to that person.*[19]

Blumhardt believed deeply all his life in the power of God's
Spirit to perform miraculous healings, and saw such events very
often as faith-building signs of the coming kingdom of God.
But when people begin to approach miraculous events from the
wrong perspective, consciously or unconsciously from a point of
view primarily of self-interest, he came to think that it is better
for them not to be healed, at least for a time – to experience the
Spirit precisely in their suffering and their disability, and in this
way learn to long for the kingdom which has not yet fully arrived.
For Blumhardt, the visceral experience of the disrupting of our
desires and plans, including for our own physical health, is a form
of 'birth-pang' – a *charismatic*, albeit cruciform, experience of
the Spirit in our bodies, minds, and feelings.

Ultimately, in his view, important though healing and
miracles are as signs of the Spirit's living activity in the
world, the most reliable and important form of the Spirit's
charismatic activity – at least until the kingdom has fully
arrived in power – is in 'negative', cross-shaped experiences.
Blumhardt's pneumatology fully allows for the power and
importance of charismatic experience of the Spirit – indeed,
he was quite sceptical of Christians who were not interested in
such experiences – but it also takes very seriously the sorts of
concerns about 'egoism' and self-deception we saw in Luther.
Blumhardt's example shows that it is indeed possible to engage
deeply with the accusation that charismatic pneumatology is

---

19 Christoph Friedrich Blumhardt, *Meine Lieben Freunde und Bekannten*. Mårz 1894,
(Bad Boll: 1894), p. 3.

dangerously prone to self-deception, while remaining robustly oriented towards visceral, miraculous, transformative, and affective experience of the Spirit.

THE CREATIVE FREEDOM OF THE SPIRIT

Prioritising this aspect of the Spirit's work has wider implications for Christian pneumatology, beyond the addressing of perhaps the most important critique of charismatic approaches to the Spirit. In the space that remains, I would like to focus on just one: the freedom of the Spirit, and its corollary in spontaneous creative activity.

A major pneumatological theme for Blumhardt is the freedom of the Spirit in relation to human expectations. His favourite way of describing this freedom is in terms of a critique of 'systems' or 'mechanisms':

It is a mistake when people believe that the Holy Spirit goes along naturally with human mechanisms and traditions. This view turns the Spirit of God into nothing more than an amplification of human opinions, so that every 'christian' phenomenon ends up being viewed by its proponents as a work of the Spirit, even if it is wrapped up in the most monstrous superstition.[20]

Elsewhere, Blumhardt summarises this freedom more succinctly, drawing on 1 Thessalonians 5:2: 'God's intervention comes much more like a thief in the night.'[21]

The scope of his critique here includes the 'means of grace' of the sacraments[22] and the Bible, as well as theology, healing

---

20 Blumhardt, *Gedanken*, p. 176.
21 Blumhardt, *Gedanken*, p. 47.
22 See for example Blumhardt, *Seid Auferstandene!*, pp. 152, 179.

ministries like his own, confessional dogma, and ecclesial structures. 'God is all sorts of things, just not a system ... Wherever people have made a religion into a system, that religion is always distant from God.'[23]

Blumhardt's critique of 'systems' captures key features of his pneumatology. The first is the unsurprisingly 'charismatic' conclusion that the Spirit's direct action in the world is not restricted to sacrament or Bible. Both *can be*, and often are, instruments through which the Spirit works, but Blumhardt is deeply critical of traditional Protestant and Roman Catholic views that God has chosen to give his Spirit to the inner person through certain specific external instruments only.

Secondly, Blumhardt's theology of the freedom of the Spirit, like his 'birth-pangs' principle, is grounded to a significant degree in his low view of human nature. If God only worked through the Spirit in certain. ways, and through specific, predictable instruments, the door would be left open for superstition and idolatry. In Blumhardt's view of human nature, people are always trying to escape having to face the living reality of God, because encounter with that living reality entails judgement and being pulled out of comfortable spiritual habits. If people believe they can secure God's blessings, especially eternal life, through sacraments, reading the Bible, going to church, adhering to a specific theological confession, or other 'usual tracks,'[24] they will do these things in place of engaging directly with the Spirit. 'Instead of using the gifts that have been given to look forwards, in order to attain the final goal, people instead turn around and marvel at the gifts, and ultimately make an idol out of them.'[25]

---

23 Blumhardt, *Gedanken*, pp. 57–58.
24 Blumhardt, *Gedanken*, p. 39.
25 Blumhardt, *Gedanken*, p. 116

Taken alone, Blumhardt's insistence on the freedom of the Spirit over and against human attempts to anticipate where, when, and how it will act can come close to a dangerous pneumatological arbitrariness. For example, would it be idolatrous systematising to say that the Spirit always acts out of love? Or that as the 'Spirit of truth' it cannot lie? Upon closer examination, however, Blumhardt's pneumatology is less arbitrary than it might appear. He cautions strongly against anticipating where and how the Spirit will act not because the Spirit is *capricious* but because human beings tend nearly always to expect the Spirit in the *wrong places*. In Blumhardt's theology, the statement, 'The Spirit blows wherever it pleases' (John 3:8), means first and foremost that the Spirit does not necessarily blow where *we* choose.

Blumhardt's understanding of the freedom of the Spirit is much more than just a critique of human desires to fit God into a clear and manageable 'system', however. The other side of that critique is the implication that God's Spirit acts in ways that are always deeply *creative*. This is no static or lifeless or 'out of touch' God, repeating the same old statements and activities over and over. Rather, the Spirit is constantly bursting into the world in unexpected and life-giving ways, inspiring people and movements, kindling affections, bringing old truths and practices to life again, and creatively destroying the obstacles we put in the way of God's kingdom. The 'negative' side, the presence of the Spirit in the disruption of comfortable patterns, simultaneously leads the way for God to act in gloriously spontaneous, vital ways, in unusual places and through surprising instruments – the rural backwater of Nazareth instead of the grandeur of Rome, fishermen instead of kings, a mixed-race working-class congregation at Azusa Street in 1906 instead of a powerful, mainline denomination, the spiritual simplicity and wonder of children preferred to the religious sophistication of adults. To take an example from Blumhardt, in his context this meant finding the Spirit relieving the plight of the working class through the very unexpected means of an (in those days) *atheistic* Social Democratic Party rather than through traditional church structures or even a 'christianised' socialist party.

What might this mean for us, to be encountered and caught off guard by what David Ford calls 'signs' of the Spirit?[26] In the superabundance of possible examples, I will limit myself to just two. The first is that it might mean finding parables of forgiveness and mercy, and the goodness of God, in unexpected places in the culture around us. One of the most exciting Christian resources I know of right now is Mockingbird Ministries, which specialises in smart, deeply felt interpretation of and openness to just such creative signs of the Spirit in secular popular culture.[27] Another expression of the Spirit's creative freedom and spontaneity, another 'sign' I have witnessed recently, has been in the unexpected friendships, intellectual insights, and spiritual connections with adherents of other faiths that have arisen through the inter-faith practice of Scriptural Reasoning, which involves Muslims, Christians, and Jews meeting regularly to read each other's scriptures together.[28] The activity of the Christian Holy Spirit through Muslim and Jewish individuals and texts has been at the same time both unexpected and astonishingly fruitful.

The Bible associates the Spirit with freedom in no uncertain terms. The Spirit itself is irreducibly free to 'blow wherever

---

26 See David F. Ford's discussion in Chapter 3 of this volume.
27 See for example, Mockingbird's recent publication *The Gospel According to Pixar*, a book that doubles as a teaching series for churches, and their booklet *Grace in Addiction: What the Church Can Learn from Alcoholics Anonymous*. For these and other resources, as well as the well-known blog, see the Mockingbird website, www.mbird.com.
28 For an introduction to Scriptural Reasoning, see www.scripturalreasoning.org. For academic reflections on it, see especially *The Promise of Scriptural Reasoning*, ed. David F. Ford and C. C. Pecknold (Oxford: Blackwell Publishers, 2006).

it pleases' (John 3:8), and in turn grants this freedom to us – 'where the Spirit of the Lord is, there is freedom' (2 Corinthians 3:17). The corollary of this freedom is the Spirit's enormous spontaneous creative power. The Spirit is associated with God's creative activity right from the start of the Bible (Genesis 1:1–3). Often, this creative work follows directly from, and is intertwined with, the Spirit's 'negative' work in judgement and the uncomfortable clearing away of ossified expectations and patterns (John 16:8), as Christoph Blumhardt understood so well. One way this 'negative' work is united with the creative work is in the fact that when the Spirit gives life, it tends often to do so particularly to *dead things* – to people and situations and needs and words beyond the reach of conventional hopes and conventional powers, like the dry bones in Ezekiel which are made alive by the breath of God (Ezekiel 37:5–6), and the quickening of our 'mortal bodies' by the Spirit described in Romans 8:11. It is especially to these dead and ossified things that the psalmist seems to be speaking in one of the most remarkable summary verses on the work of the Spirit, Psalm 104:30: 'When you send forth your Spirit, they are created; and you renew the face of the ground.'

9 PNEUMATOLOGY, HEALING AND POLITICAL POWER: SKETCHING A PENTECOSTAL POLITICAL THEOLOGY

LUKE BRETHERTON

Pentecostal and charismatic churches do not have a good reputation when it comes to politics. Frequent criticisms levelled at them include: they legitimate and collude with neo-liberal ideologies and represent a form of capitalism-friendly Christianity; they are quietist and inward looking, being so heavenly focused they are no earthly good; they are naive and easily co-opted by authoritarian regimes as a counterbalance to more socially and politically critical churches; their emphasis on spiritual warfare lends itself to demonising and scapegoating political opponents, so transforming secular economic and political conflicts of interest into cosmic struggles between good and evil.[1]

There is some truth to all these criticisms; but it is neither the whole truth nor a necessary and inevitable state of affairs. As

---

1 For some examples of this see Amos Yong, *In the Days of Caesar: Pentecostalism and Political Theology* (Grand Rapids, MI: Eerdmans, 2010), pp. 131–134.

Donald Miller and Tetsunao Yamamori suggest in their study of worldwide Pentecostal and charismatic churches, counter examples of what they call 'progressive Pentecostalism' are as readily apparent.[2] On their account, Pentecostalism is a vibrant movement of social transformation among the poorest and most marginalised communities around the world. David Martin's sociological studies of Pentecostalism in Latin America confirm this. Martin argues that it is Pentecostal churches rather than those influenced by Liberation theologies that are transforming the barrios of Latin America for the better.[3] Theologically, the voices of Pentecostal theologians are starting to reckon with the political witness of Pentecostal and charismatic churches.[4] Reflections on such phenomena as glossolalia, exorcism, and ecstatic worship are taken as the beginning point for developing a distinctive Pentecostal political theology. Such voices represent a counter to the 'cultured despisers' of Pentecostalism.

What follows is a reflection on healing, both as a theological category and as a phenomenon. This reflection is a way of sketching a Pentecostal political theology that is itself an act of healing and repair of what are judged to be theologically impoverished or mistaken conceptualisations of the relationship between faithful witness and political practice. This act of repair is addressed to a category central to the self-understanding of the Pentecostal and charismatic movements. Belief in Jesus as healer was one of the fourfold holiness doctrines adopted by classical Pentecostals into their theology. As Amos Yong argues,

2 Donald Miller and Tetsunao Yamamori, *Global Pentecostalism: The New Face of Christian Social Engagement* (Berkeley: University of California Press, 2007).
3 David Martin, *Pentecostalism: The World Their Parish* (Oxford: Blackwell Publishers, 2002).
4 Foremost among these is Amos Yong's *In the Days of Caesar*. See also James K. A. Smith, '"The spirits of the prophets are subject to the prophets": Global Pentecostalism and the Re-enchantment of Critique', *South Atlantic Quarterly* 109.4 (2010), pp. 677–693.

for Pentecostals, Jesus' healing ministry is part of the atonement, the reason being that if 'the work of Christ reversed the effects of the fall with regard to the nature of sin, then it did so with regard to the nature of sickness and disease'.[5] A central claim of Pentecostal and charismatic theology is that the same Spirit who healed through Jesus continues to work today. However, what is less reflected upon is the theo-political dynamics of this emphasis on healing. I want to suggest that without attention to the theo-political dynamics inherent in acts of healing, the nature of healing itself cannot be properly understood.

What will not be proposed is that healing is the basis for constructing a whole account of the social and political witness of the church. What follows is the more modest proposal that healing is part of a repertoire of acts by which God establishes a community that can bear faithful witness to the coming kingdom. Following the pattern of Christ's life, death and resurrection, healing is an event that simultaneously ruptures and repairs the world so that it both experiences and is reopened to its true end: the eschatological communion of creation and God.

HEALING AS THEO-POLITICAL EVENT

In the Gospels, Jesus is either moved to heal by compassion and mercy (eg Matthew 20:34; 15:32; 9:36, and Luke 7:13) or in response to a request for him to have compassion or mercy (eg Mark 9:22; Luke 17:13; Matthew 9:27; 15:22 and 17:15). He heals those who have need and Jesus' acts of healing are personal and particular, occasioned by paying close attention to who is before him. A contrast can be drawn here between Jesus' acts of healing and political policies and ideologies that seek to address human need not one person at a time but all

---

5 Yong, *In the Days of Caesar*, p. 259.

at once, through one size fits all procedures and programmes. Healing, after the pattern of Jesus, is a relational, interpersonal act, encompassing not only a divine – human relation, but also a human-to-human act, as the person healed is listened to, prayed for and celebrated as part of the process of healing. The outcome of this process is not simply physical or emotional but social: healing enables deeper personal presence and participation in the communion of divine and human relations.

The motivation for the response or request for healing is a deep sense of grief that the world is not as it should be. The compassion evoked in Jesus is not born out of an abstract sense of obligation or duty to do the right thing. Neither is healing an act of *noblesse oblige* by the privileged on behalf of the less fortunate. Rather, compassion is the beginning point of receptivity, an openness and hearing of the other and entering into their experience. Compassion necessitates listening and in listening we refuse to exclude the other; instead we locate them as a participant in a common world of meaning and action. Listening both presumes a common realm of shared action and meaning and is an act that intends and embodies such a realm.[6]

Healing as an expression of compassion has an apophatic

---

6 Compassion is understood here to be a form of suffering or pathos that responds not on the basis of a predetermined policy or rule, or an ideologically fixed picture of what is the case, but through listening to, receiving and being affected by the need of another. To frame this in terms of virtue ethics, compassion is an expression of the virtue of *misericordia*. As Alasdair MacIntyre defines it, *misericordia* denotes the capacity for grief or sorrow over someone else's distress, just insofar as one understands the other's distress as one's own. It is not mere sentiment; instead, it is sentiment guided by reason. Following Aquinas' definition of the term, he states: '*Misericordia* is that aspect of charity whereby we supply what is needed by our neighbour and among the virtues that relate us to our neighbour *misericordia* is the greatest.' Alasdair MacIntyre, *Dependent Rational Animals: Why Human Beings Need the Virtues* (London: Duckworth, 1999), p. 125. For MacIntyre, to understand another's distress as one's own is to recognise that other as a neighbour, whether they are family, a friend, or a stranger. Thus, *misericordia* directs one to include the stranger within one's communal relationships. It is thus the basis for extending the bounds of one's communal obligations, and thereby including the other in one's relations of giving and receiving characterised by just generosity.

beginning: it demands we empty ourselves of our predetermined judgements about who is before us and allow perception of the world around us to form through an act of compassionate reception rather than acting on some established notion or idea about how the world should look. This is the point of tension in many of Jesus' acts of healing, most pointedly articulated in John 9 when Jesus heals the man born blind. Jesus refuses the predetermination of the man's status as sinner or a son of sinners. In doing so, he refuses the rationalisations of inequality, social exclusion and oppression that those around him regurgitate. Instead, he sees the man as a subject of God, through whom God's sovereign rule will be displayed: 'Jesus answered, "Neither this man nor his parents sinned; he was born blind so that God's works might be revealed in him."'

Jesus' act of healing itself throws the local community and the worldview of its leaders into an epistemic crisis as it challenges their received wisdom: that is, it profoundly challenges and disorientates their view of the world. A measure of the depth of the crisis is that the healed man's neighbours don't recognise him (verse 9): remember, nothing about him has changed except that he can now see. And the Pharisees are thrown into turmoil, eventually refusing to believe he was ever blind rather than face the cognitive dissonance the act of healing raises for them (verse 18). The key contrast is between Jesus, who pays attention to the man as he is, and the Pharisees, who do not listen or take seriously the need of the man in order to uphold their ideological framework. Likewise, Jesus' acts of healing on the Sabbath draw out the contrast between those who refuse to act because of a legalistic rule or programme and the one who will and can act justly responding to each on the basis of their need. This can be further illustrated through the story of the healing of blind Bartimaeus (Mark 10:46–52). Bartimaeus calls to Jesus for a hearing of his case, ascribing to Jesus the status of messianic ruler 'Jesus, Son of David, have mercy on me!' (Note, this act of healing prefigures the triumphal entry of Jesus into Jerusalem and the cleansing of the temple that immediately follow on from it in Mark 11, acts in which Jesus' messianic rule is announced at the heart of political power.) In contrast to those around Bartimaeus, who rebuke him, Jesus stops and listens, then calls Bartimaeus forth from his position of marginality and exclusion. Hearing his case, Jesus judges by healing Bartimaeus. But this healing judgement is not a unilateral pronouncement, but comes through dialogic encounter, and the healing itself is a divine – human event in which Bartimaeus is the primary actor.

However, we only see half the miracle if we focus on the restoration of sight to Bartimaeus. The event of healing Mark depicts has a double aspect. Its first aspect is the restoration of sight to the blind. Its second aspect is the opening of the eyes of those around Bartimaeus so they would pay attention to him, seeing him in a new light and not dismiss and marginalise him or others like him. The fruit of these two aspects of the event of healing is the challenging of systemic patterns of exclusions, the inclusion of the excluded and the reorientation of the excluders.

As in the story of Bartimaeus, healing converts private suffering and individual compassion into a public enactment of judgement against the world as it is by unveiling the eschatological possibilities of the world as God intends it to be. In contrast to prayer and acts of giving, where Jesus counsels secrecy – not letting the right hand know what the left is doing – acts of healing are public works that disrupt and challenge the ruling status quo. In short, healing is intrinsically a theo-political event. As illustrated by the healing of the man with the withered hand (Mark 3:1–6), Jesus' acts of healing are not simply individual acts of mercy, but unveil the inadequacy and hardness of heart of those in power, who are shown to be without compassion and unable to respond to the basic needs and dignity of those they claim authority over. Moreover, the power of those in control is seen to be as nothing to the power of God revealed in Jesus. Healing reveals a power that can constructively regenerate and renew the world: it can restore sight, heal a withered hand, and even raise the dead. The power of the ruling elites is, by contrast, either shown to be ineffectual, unconcerned or simply destructive: it is the power of the sword that can threaten, imprison and crucify but cannot encourage, heal or resurrect.[7]

In sum, healing, as a theo-political act, is a summons to those with authority to listen first, to have mercy and not be hard hearted, and to recognise and take responsibility for the limits and nature of their power.

HEALING AS SOCIAL EVENT

Jesus' critique of the impotency of the rulers of his day echoes the Prophets critique of poor rule and the Old Testament ideal of the just ruler. This ideal is set out in Job 29:7–25, where Job states that as a ruler he robed himself in justice and that his defence of the weak and needy included being 'eyes to the blind, and feet to the lame'. Likewise, Psalm 146:7–9 describes God as one who does justice for the oppressed, who include the blind. In the Old Testament, physical malady is explicitly linked with economic, political and social injustice. This was for good reason. Physical affliction was an economic, social and political

---

7 The nature of the threat was clearly understood by those with a vested interest in maintaining the status quo (including those who claimed to oppose it but whose authority was based not on presenting a real alternative, as Jesus did, but on an oppositional identity that was locked in a negative mimesis with that which it opposed). This secret solidarity between self-proclaimed opposition and established political elite is drawn out in Mark 3:6 after Jesus heals the man with the withered hand: 'The Pharisees went out and immediately conspired with the Herodians against him, how to destroy him.'

catastrophe.[8] As Richard Wilkinson and Kate Pickett make clear in their research on inequality, the same is true today.[9] The rich live longer, are less sick and convert economic power into political power in order to secure their interests. Conversely, ill health or being disabled are directly correlated with poverty and political impotency.

The physically sick and disabled are lacking in power to maintain themselves and are unable to participate in the common world of meaning and action that constitutes the body politic. The role of the ruler is literally to make them strong by defending their interests and empowering them to act for themselves.[10] God's coming justice necessarily brings healing as part of a wider ushering in of a just and righteous social, political and economic order. For example, after the acclamation in Isaiah 33:22 that 'The Lord is our judge, the Lord is our ruler, the Lord is our king; he will save us,' the passage continues in verse 24, 'And no inhabitant will say, "I am sick".' Folding these Old Testament themes into it, the announcement of Jesus' mission in Luke 4 is portrayed as the fulfilment of the messianic hope for a just and righteous ruler whose raising up of the lowly includes physical healing (Luke 4:18–19).

Physical healing is part of the challenging of social exclusion and the structural conditions that keep the poor poor. Healing challenges exclusion and impoverishment by showing forth a contrary social, political and economic logic. It represents a contradiction by forming a common world of meaning and action with those who are excluded. The formation of such a world entails the breaking down of those structures and patterns

---

8   Stephen Charles Mott, 'Our Biblical Call to Healing.' Paper presented to the Free Methodist Medical Fellowship, 26 September 2003.
9   Richard G Wilkinson. and Kate Pickett, *The Spirit Level: Why More Equal Societies Almost Always Do Better* (London: Allen Lane, 2009).
10 Ezekiel 34 portrays the dereliction of this duty.

of relationship that exclude vulnerable strangers: the lame and the blind. Healing summons forth those excluded into a public or common life by enacting an event of divine – human communion – literally, the joining of Spirit and flesh in the process of healing – thereby communicating to the excluded that they are not rejected, abandoned or forgotten, and announcing to the excluders that the sick or disabled are subjects of divine blessing, not wrath. The primary achievement of healing is not the restoration of sight or the ability to walk, but the restoration of the ability of those healed to express themselves within and act upon a common world, in which walking and seeing symbolise the basic requirements of active participation. As Tom Wright puts it: 'Jesus' healing miracles must be seen clearly as bestowing the gift of *shalom*, wholeness, to those who lacked it, bringing not only physical health but renewed membership in the people of YHWH.'[11] On this account, physical healing is one kind of outcome, but the witness of a community such as L'Arche, which establishes community between the able-bodied and severely disabled, is a more powerful testimony still to the healing power of the Spirit.

We misunderstand what healing is for if we individualise it and focus on its physical or immediate outcomes. Healing is given, like all gifts of God, for the building up of the body of Christ. It is yet another way in which the Spirit acts among us to form a social body that bears witness to God's coming kingdom. It is not a fruit of the Spirit, but is given to enable us to bear the fruits of the Spirit that find their fulfilment and purpose in divine – human communion. Healing is a way in which the Spirit reforms, reweaves and reconstitutes relationships so as to be communion-like. Through acts of healing, we learn to see, hear and walk more faithfully with God and each other. But

---

11 N. T. Wright, *Jesus and the Victory of God* (London: SPCK, 1996), p. 192.

as an event and sign, an act of healing is necessarily singular and particular. Jesus does not heal everyone all at once, but one or two, here and there. If the primary aim of healing is not the physical transformation of the individual, but the social transformation of exclusionary or destructive or idolatrous patterns of relationship, then healing will only be occasional. Sometimes we can learn what we need to by other means. And sometimes, healing would be counterproductive. Russell Rook tells a helpful story that illustrates what I am trying to say here.

Two years ago now, Nicola, the pastor of my local church died. Since then, I've often reflected on her death. She had suffered from cancer for eighteen months. Obviously, as an evangelical charismatic church, we prayed for healing many, many times, but somewhere along the way, we got to a point at the end when we began to prepare for her death rather than simply expect a miraculous healing to happen. Having lived very well, Nicola died very well, and, in this, she taught us more as a church than we ever could have learned through a miraculous healing. I had the privilege of joining the family for a few hours on that last afternoon. Around her bedside, family and friends sat singing songs, telling stories, praying, laughing, crying. None of this is to underestimate the pain of Nicola's death for the many people who loved and mourned her, but in that hospital room, I discovered ... that in Christ, death has lost its sting ... There was something about Nicola's death that taught us to learn to live hopefully, and it was only her death that could have done it. A miraculous healing would not have taught us to live hopefully ever after. It would have only increased the modern illusion that we can cheat death, whether by the modern marvels of medical science or a prayer for healing. Once again, I don't offer this theological observation glibly as I know that, in her absence, Nicola's

139

*family and friends continue to pay an enormous price for the
lesson that she has taught.*[12]

Healing bears witness to the now/not yet nature of the kingdom
Christ establishes. Healing makes tangible the transformed
social reality that the power of God enables in the life of the
believer and believing community. Yet, as an indicative act of
communication, it simultaneously unveils the presence and the
absence of God. The act of healing manifests the power and
victory of Christ in the one who is healed, while simultaneously
revealing the absence of God's power in these unhealed others.
While suffering makes palpable the boundary between God and
the world in his absence, healing suspends this boundary and
makes God's presence known. The entirety of God's revelation
is thus made possible in the event of healing. The response to
healing must combine resurrection gladness with cruciform
lament at the ongoing suffering and incompleteness of the
healing of creation. To condemn churches that emphasise healing
as triumphalist or as having an over-realised eschatology may
be to correctly question their poorly conceived eschatology, but
it should not be assumed that an emphasis on healing leads
inevitably to triumphalism. Healing in its very particularity
bears witness to the now/not yet eschatological tension.

HEALING AS ASSOCIATIVE POWER THAT ENACTS AND EXTENDS GOD'S RULE

Healing as a manifestation of the redeeming power of God is
part of God's initiatory action to re-enable action by others
where the effects of sin and death have disabled common action

---

12 Luke Bretherton and Russell Rook, eds, *Living Out Loud: Conversations about Virtue,
Ethics & Evangelicalism* (Milton Keynes: Paternoster Press, 2010), p. 152.

in pursuit of good ends. Miroslav Volf names the distorted forms of relationship that sin and death reproduce, 'exclusion'. Exclusion is destructive of creation because it either cuts good connections, breaking down interdependence, so the 'other' emerges as an enemy (eg competitive individualism); or erases separation, not recognising the 'other' as someone who, in his or her otherness, belongs to the pattern of interdependence. The other then emerges as an inferior who must either be assimilated to be like me or subjugated to me (eg colonialism). Exclusion is the false setting of boundaries and the exploding of proper ones, pushing creation back to chaos.[13] Healing is part of the creative work of the Spirit in separating and binding together that which has been exploded and imploded by sin and death. However, healing is given not for one's own advancement or personal blessing but to bear witness to and enable the formation of a common life. The piling up of spiritual blessing, like the piling up of money unspent on the good of others, is anathema to true healing. As already noted, the gift received must be reinvested in building up the body of Christ. Or as Paul puts it in 1 Corinthians 12:7: 'To each is given the manifestation of the Spirit for the common good.'

The Spirit enables the disempowered to stop being subjects of others' actions on them, a position that renders them always having to react or be passive. We can contrast healing with paternalistic forms of welfare provision that take away the ability of others to act for themselves, despite the fact that paternalism seeks to act helpfully on their behalf. The paternalistic provision of charity maintains the unequal distribution of power and denies the excluded responsible, active agency in a common world. In effect, it reproduces patterns of exclusion

---

13 Miroslav Volf, *Exclusion and Embrace: A Theological Exploration of Identity, Otherness, and Reconciliation* (Nashville, TN: Abingdon Press, 1996).

while claiming to empower. Healing is an anti-paternalistic act that establishes non-instrumental, non-pecuniary, reciprocal relations. It enacts the possibility of an economy of blessing where power is distributed outside conditions of conflict and scarcity because the power it draws on is unlimited and eternal. Thus, as a social – material event, healing challenges processes of exclusion, marginalisation and injustice, re-establishing reciprocal relations that constitute the basis of relational forms of power. Such relational power contrasts with unilateral forms of power that dominate and disaggregate social life.

HEALING AS JUDGEMENT

Healing as a theo-political act addresses the dual socio-political and spiritual dynamics of the principalities and powers. Healing as an act of compassion that challenges injustice through enacting God's *shalom* constitutes both the promulgation of God's judgement against the principalities and powers and a proleptic disclosure of their redemption.[14] Healing points to the ongoing purification and reordering of the powers in the present age and the possibility of their ultimate renovation in the age to come. As Oliver O'Donovan notes: 'Jesus' *works of power* (*dunameis*) were identified in the Gospel tradition as acts of exorcism and healing. They were taken to be victories over the demonic powers.'[15] That we cannot view Jesus' acts of

---

14 I do not have space here to rehearse the debate about the nature of the principalities and powers. This debate centres on two questions: first, do the principalities and powers refer solely to material structural dynamics or to cosmic, extra-material forces; and second, are the powers redeemable or not? For a helpful review of this debate in biblical studies and political theology see Yong, *In the Days of Caesar,* pp. 129–151. I take the view that the principalities and powers mentioned in Luke – Acts and the Pauline epistles are both spiritual and socio-political and are created good, presently fallen, judged in the Christ-event, and open to redemption at the eschatological fulfilment of all things.
15 Oliver O'Donovan, *The Desire of the Nations: Rediscovering the Roots of Political*

exorcism and healing as acts of political power reflects more on our narrowed conception of politics than on the actions of Christ. O'Donovan suggests that Jesus' seeming lack of concern about the colonial oppression of Rome reflects a theological analysis of the true predicament of Israel and its thoroughly depoliticised and disaggregated condition. What Israel needed was not revolution but reconstitution as a people capable of acting together in pursuit of its real interests. O'Donovan argues that Jesus' acts of healing and exorcism represented a new source of power, one that:

> *was directed against the forces which most immediately hindered Israel from living effectively as a community in God's service, the spiritual and natural weaknesses which drained its energies away. This was not an apolitical gesture, but a statement of true political priorities. Jesus' departure from the zealot programme showed his more theological understanding of power, not his disinterest in it. The empowerment of Israel was more important than the disempowerment of Rome; for Rome disempowered would in itself by no means guarantee Israel empowered ... The power which God gave to Israel did not have to be taken from ... Rome first. The gift of power was not a zero sum operation. God could generate new power by doing new things in Israel's midst.[16]*

Healing and exorcism speak of a power greater and more generative than that available to earthly political authorities.[17]

Theory (Cambridge: Cambridge University Press, 1996), p. 93.

16 *op. cit.*, p. 95.

17 For a parallel reading in relation to exorcism see Richard Horsley, *Jesus and Empire: The Kingdom of God and the New World Disorder* (Fortress Press, 2002). For example, Horsley states: 'The series of episodes in which Jesus exorcises demons and the discussions of the significance of Jesus' exorcisms in the Gospels indicate that precisely

It is a power that is dependent on God, not on humankind or possibilities inherent in creation. Indeed, Jesus focuses on miracles because miracles relativise political power and show up its impotence: all the training and power of the centurion cannot heal his child; only his faith can. Through his acts of healing, Jesus was restating that liberation from that which enslaves us, whether it be political or natural, is ultimately dependent on God. At the same time, Jesus was demonstrating his rulership and establishing his arena of rule, a rule that far exceeded the reach and power of Rome. The sphere of God's active rule involved the redeeming and perfecting of creation. In the power of the Spirit, Jesus initiates and illustrates this rule in exorcisms, calming storms, and healings. In all this, Jesus is demonstrating how the present state of things relates to reality as being established by God. What Jesus does and says acts as an invitation to anticipate now what will be the case in the coming kingdom. Washing feet and crucifixion spell out the nature of the king and his rule, while raising up the lowly and bringing down the proud, filling the hungry with good things, and letting the oppressed go free constitutes the pattern of life that is to be lived in this kingdom (Luke 1:51–55; 4:18–19). As Stephen Mott notes: 'Healing is part of a continuum of actions of deliverance from forces which deny people's basic needs for life in community.'[18]

HEALING AS ECCLESIAL ACT

In the synoptic gospels the disciples are sent out to do that for which Jesus was sent. In Luke 9:2 the twelve are sent to 'proclaim the kingdom of God and to heal' and in Luke 10 the

---

in his practice of exorcism God's kingdom is defeating Roman rule.' *Ibid*, p. 99.
18 Mott, 'Our Biblical Call to Healing,' p. 16.

seventy are sent out and instructed to 'cure the sick who are there, and say to them, "The kingdom of God has come near to you."' The new community Jesus establishes is to carry on his ministry and is authorised to act in the same power. Through the Spirit, this power is available to all. Building on the work of Max Turner, Amos Yong argues that:

The saving, sanctifying, and empowering works of the Spirit produce a new body politic, one in which socio-economic, class, ethnic, and gender differences are leveled out in a variety of ways. Hence Jesus' mission to renew and restore Israel is continued in and through the church, except that the chasm between Jew and gentile has now been bridged by the outpouring of the Spirit on all flesh (Acts 2:17), with the result that the gentiles of the world have now been invited to participate in the redemption of Israel.[19]

Healing is not only an act that promulgates God's rule but, in the power of the Spirit, it creates a social body where Christ's rule is experienced. Healing reconstitutes the subject as someone under divine rule, physically inscribing his or her body with the power of God. Against those who posit an antithesis between flesh and Spirit, healing enacts the Pauline understanding of the relationship between them. For Paul, the fleshly life refers to that pattern of life that is oriented towards death and disintegration because it is moving away from communion with God. By contrast, life empowered by the Spirit is one re-oriented and enabled to pursue and fulfil communion with God and undertake the kinds of social, economic and political relationships that eschatologically inhabit this communion. It is a work of the Spirit who is the one who brings creation into

---

19 Yong, *In the Days of Caesar*, p. 106.

being, who enables God to be incarnate: that is to say, it is part of the Spirit's work of enabling true materiality, materiality in and through Christ. This materiality is *shalom* or kingdom-like in its outworking. Healing is a manifestation of the Spirit's work in forming a social body that bears witness to divine rule.

The relationship between healing and the formation of the church as a socio-political body can be illustrated through contemporary experience. Omar McRoberts, in his ethnographic study of Pentecostal churches in Boston, suggests that during times of ecstatic worship:

> *the 'cosmic power' referred to in preaching and testimony reveals itself to believers not just as a rhetorical move but as actual power that descends into the room and demonstrates its ability to level social distinctions. Migrant churches used this ritual levelling not to separate members from the world but to affirm their ability to operate, however cautiously and selectively, in the world.*[20]

In McRoberts's view, ecstatic worship and healing was a way in which marginalised and poor groups built up a social body among those who are constantly broken down as individuals and disaggregated and disorganised as a community by the power of the market and state acting against them. The demand that families and neighbourhoods are broken up and migrate in order to serve the flows of capital, goods and services is countered by the flow of the Spirit which reconstitutes a social body in particular places that has the power to heal and act together for its own good – in the first instance through 'inreach' – and then in pursuit of the common good through 'outreach'.

---

20 Omar Maurice McRoberts, *Streets of Glory: Church and Community in a Black Urban Neighborhood* (Chicago: University of Chicago Press, 2003), p. 104.

Healing opens up a space within the world as it is so that the world can be encountered as an open system capable of radical change. As Yong comments:

Pentecostal worship ... carves out political space and enables a new political identity to emerge over social space and social time among pentecostal communities. In the global south, especially, observe how pentecostal liturgical practices dominate their weekly rhythms, in terms of putting believers in church five to seven nights (or days) a week; how weekly, monthly, or quarterly all-night prayer meetings and their concomitant seasons of fasting shape the pentecostal expectation of divine provision in a hostile polis; and how the intensity of pentecostal praise and worship is a public expression of an alternative community consisting of brothers and sisters in Christ through the Spirit. With these practices, pentecostals are not only engaging with God, but also with the spiritual realm of the principalities and powers – taking authority over the turmoil in their personal lives, the devastations of their economies, and the challenges in the public domain.[21]

Healing does not, however, create dependency. It does not produce a docile or passive body. Against the kind of 'drain' metaphor sometimes deployed to describe praying for healing, which suggests humans are simply inert vehicles for the work of the Spirit, healing does not do for others what they can do for themselves. It is a summons to take responsibility and to act within the common world, within which the healed now participate. This is constantly reiterated in the Gospels. 'Stand up, take your mat and walk' (John 5:8), 'Go, wash' (John

---

21 Yong, *In the Days of Caesar*. p. 156.

9:7), 'Go home to your friends, and tell them how much the Lord has done for you, and what mercy he has shown you' (Mark 5:19): these are not the expressions of one who acts unilaterally expecting nothing in return, but of one who seeks relationship and expects a response. The altar call could be seen as a contemporary equivalent. The point here is that against the depoliticised condition of Israel or marginalised communities in the global South, the Spirit distributes power so that people can act for themselves within a common world of speech and action, that is the church. Healing is both a political act that builds up and restores the people of God and a Spirit-filled act that mediates the work of God in the world.

HEALING AS DIVINE – HUMAN LABOUR

As a public work of the people of God and a work of the Spirit within the world, healing is a mutual or common divine – human labour. As a form of labour it represents a non-monetised, unalienated form of work outside the formal economy and, as with its relation to political power, it unveils the impotence and hardness of heart of the power of money and the market. As a response to the domination of Israel by the power of money through taxation and usury, acts of healing by Jesus and the apostles should be read as part of the declaration of Jubilee. The declaration of Jubilee – that is, the release from debt slavery – forms the basis of how Luke frames Jesus' announcement of his purpose and mission (Luke 4:18–19).[22] And what Luke then depicts in Acts 2 is the enactment of the Jubilee community

---

22 For an extended reading of this text as a declaration of Jubilee see John Howard Yoder, *The Politics of Jesus*, 2nd ed. (Grand Rapids, MA: Eerdmans, 1994), pp. 60–75. Yoder includes the Lord's Prayer as a call for the proper practice of Jubilee with its use of the word *aphiemi* in the statement: 'remit us our debts as we ourselves have also remitted them to our debtors', *Ibid*, p. 62.

where healing, signs and wonders and freedom from debt and material want are envisaged as fruits of the Pentecostal outpouring: 'Awe came upon everyone, because many wonders and signs were being done by the apostles. All who believed were together and had all things in common; they would sell their possessions and goods and distribute the proceeds to all, as any had need' (Acts 2:43–45). Deliverance from debt-slavery is intertwined with deliverance from physical bondage as signs of the empowering presence of the Spirit.

And here we return to the problem of poor practice outlined in the criticisms made of Pentecostal and charismatic churches at the outset of this chapter. In the contemporary context, where the formal economy and public life are dominated by capitalism and a post-Enlightenment worldview, healing is part of the informal economy and a contraband worldview. It is unofficial, unregulated, untaxed, highly entrepreneurial, and dependent on social networks and mutual solidarity. Hence exploitation and racketeering are endemic to the practice of healing which, like other parts of this outlaw world (prostitution and drug trafficking being paradigm examples) exists separated from the bureaucratised, rational and managed sectors of economic and political life. Yet at the same time, as Yong suggests, participation 'in the informal economy serves as a protest against the self-interested greed, consumerist materialism, and rampant hedonism that perennially threaten to undermine the market economy.'[23]

CONCLUSION

To conclude, healing is a theo-political event that bears witness to and promulgates Christ's eschatological rule. As a theo-political

---

23 Yong, *In the Days of Caesar*, p. 308.

event, it is an act of judgement against the hardness of heart and destructive effects of the political and economic powers. But as a divine judgement, it condemns by creatively forging a contradiction to the exclusionary and dominatory logics of worldly political and economic power. That contradiction is the church and the social, political and economic practices that bear faithful witness to the coming kingdom of God.

10 Pneumatology and the New Testament

Chris Tilling

The title of this chapter is deliberately not 'New Testament Pneumatology', but rather 'Pneumatology and the New Testament'. There are superficial reasons for this: first, and to put it bluntly, there is no single, simple pneumatology to which all authors of the New Testament adhere. Indeed, New Testament scholars have long recognised a plurality of ways of understanding the Spirit and the Spirit's activity in the pages of different New Testament authors. Perhaps it is no surprise, some may therefore think, that a book on pneumatology is best served by letting the systematicians, the Moltmanns, Volfs, and so on, have their say: anything else will get us bogged down in exegetical detail, and may even confuse more than it clarifies. And I must admit, New Testament scholars can often unhelpfully delight in trying to muddy the otherwise clear waters of systematic theological proposals!

A second, and related, superficial reason can be offered for this title: given the complex process involved in reconciling disparate New Testament voices to try to speak of a New Testament pneumatology as an integrated whole, it would require more time than is available in such a short session –

indeed I simply refer to Max Turner's brilliant book, *The Holy Spirit and Spiritual Gifts Then and Now*,[1] for those who want to begin to explore New Testament pneumatology. What can be done today, however, is to outline some of the key areas of contemporary debate concerning pneumatology and the New Testament. But there are deeper, and ultimately more important, reasons why this chapter has been given the title it has – 'Pneumatology and the New Testament' – and we will explore those reasons a little later after we have overviewed some of those key pneumatology debates.

KEY NEW TESTAMENT PNEUMATOLOGY DEBATES

In examining important debates on this topic, one must immediately reckon with the sort of reader presupposed. New Testament academics have their debates, which are often quite distinct from those entertained by church leaders, and so on. But first, let us note some of the contemporary debates in the world of New Testament academia.

Perhaps the most prominent debate concerns the various models of how the Spirit is received by or conveyed to believers. There are two main options. On the one hand are those who champion an understanding of the gift of the Spirit as something that happens in some sense *subsequent to conversion*. This may be associated with confirmation and the laying on of hands in some traditions, or the 'baptism of the Holy Spirit' in others, which may also sometimes include the laying on of hands.

In modern exegesis, Robert Menzies has argued most vigorously for a standpoint in this broad position, namely for a two-stage reception of the Spirit, first in conversion and then

---

1 Max Turner, *The Holy Spirit and Spiritual Gifts: Then and Now* (Carlisle: Paternoster, 1999).

again, *subsequent* to conversion, as an empowering for mission (compare, for example, *Empowered for Witness: The Spirit in Luke–Acts*[2]). This model relies on a harmonisation of two distinct New Testament voices. On the one hand Paul is clear: 'Anyone who does not have the Spirit of Christ does not belong to him' (Romans 8:9); 'you have received a spirit of adoption. When we cry, "Abba! Father!" it is that very Spirit bearing witness with our spirit that we are children of God' (Romans 8:15–16). Yet Luke–Acts can be interpreted in such a way that implies the Spirit is given *subsequent* to conversion, to empower Christians for ministry (and is thus not directly to be understood primarily in terms of the spiritual, ethical or religious renewal of individual Christians). So Acts 1:8 states: 'you will receive power when the Holy Spirit has come upon you; and you will be my *witnesses* in Jerusalem, in all Judea and Samaria, and to the ends of the earth.' And in Acts 19:2 Paul is reported to have asked some Ephesian 'believers' the famous question, pregnant with Spirit-reception implications: 'Did you receive the Holy Spirit when you became believers?' Taken as a whole, then, the New Testament, Menzies argues, supports a two-stage reception model.

On the other hand, many scholars argue that the Spirit is given not in two stages, but at the *beginning* of the Christian life, in the process of what James Dunn has famously called 'conversion-initiation'. This is not to rule out that a Christian may experience many fillings of the Spirit throughout the Christian life. It is to deny that a post-conversion 'baptism of the Spirit' is necessary to empower for mission, and that this second experience should be sought as a normal Christian expectation.

Indeed, Turner notes that the two-stage model of Spirit reception is not actually propounded by any one single New

---

2 Robert P. Menzies, *Empowered for Witness: The Spirit in Luke–Acts*, (JPT, Sheffield: Sheffield Academic Press, 1994).

Testament author. Paul does not speak of a subsequent reception of the Spirit for mission, and Turner challenges the notion that a post-conversion reception of the Spirit for mission is the norm even for Luke. As conversion-initiation tends to involve water baptism, some traditions emphasise that the gift of the Spirit is conveyed to the believer by the rite of water baptism (so Lampe[3]) thus paving the way for a more sacramental perspective.

The academic debate on these matters can be traced in the various exchanges between those two good friends, Robert Menzies and Max Turner. At a more popular level, the debate can be followed in the *Journal of Pentecostal Theology*, between Max Turner and David Pawson. In such a short chapter it would be wrong to take sides. But Max Turner, James Dunn and others are, as far as I can see, basically on the money! Either way, there is a strong desire among most of these scholars, whatever side of the debate they stand on, to encourage Christians to develop a deeper expectancy and hope in the presence, power and enabling of the Spirit of God today.

A particular, arguably peculiar, German tradition of New Testament scholarship has developed the sacramental line of thought to speak of the Holy Spirit as a substance. So Friedrich Wilhelm Horn has argued that, as Paul's pneumatology develops, at a certain stage Paul comes to think of the Spirit as a *substance*.[4] In response to this thesis, another German scholar, Volker Rabens, argues more persuasively that the Spirit, in Paul, should be understood not in terms of substance but in terms of God's relationality – a matter that I will explore a little more later on.[5]

---

3 G. W. H. Lampe, *The Seal of the Spirit* (London: SPCK, 1967).

4 See Friedrich Wilhelm Horn, *Das Angeld des Geistes: Studien zur paulinischen Pneumatologie* (Göttingen: Vandenhoeck & Ruprecht, 1992).

5 Volker Rabens, *The Holy Spirit and Ethics in Paul: Transformation and Empowering for Religious-Ethical Life* (Tübingen: Mohr Siebeck, 2009).

John Levison, in his recent book *Filled with the Spirit*, has raised the question to what extent the human spirit can really be distinguished from the divine Spirit.[6] He argues that the spirit received at birth is none other than the divine Spirit experienced in charismatic encounters with God, or – as he puts it with more precision at other times – the human and divine Spirit are of the same *origin* and that there is continuity between them to the point where it is almost impossible to distinguish one from another. This is a very new thesis and will, potentially, offer a third option beyond two-stage and conversion-initiation Spirit reception models, or at least open up other areas of debate.

Beyond these debates, the present rethinking of Paul and justification is potentially important for re-engaging New Testament pneumatology. There is a shift away from theological models that sharply distinguish justification, on the one hand, and the Spirit's work associated with sanctification and assurance, on the other. The former, justification (often associated with Romans 1–4), has often been understood in legal, rational, conditional and contractual terms – and has concurrently been described by some as the centre of Paul's theology. Yet this contractual stage has not cohered comfortably with the role of the Spirit, which tends to be associated more strongly with relational categories (see Rabens above), including participation in Christ and 'sanctification' (which are linked with Romans 5–8). This has arguably led some New Testament theologies to write eloquently about the centrality of justification in Paul and the New Testament, and to do so in such a way that effectively brackets out the more uncomfortably supernatural elements associated with New Testament Spirit language, a problem to which we will return at the end of this chapter.

---

6   John R. Levison, *Filled with the Spirit* (Grand Rapids, MI: Eerdmans, 2009).

Gladly, modern works on Pauline theology, especially those penned by Douglas Campbell, have seriously challenged the 'justification theory' edifice, and the justification-sanctification dichotomy has long been discredited – even if these distinctions remain in popular level understandings of Paul. The Spirit's work must be seen right at the heart of Paul's gospel, not merely as a second stage add-on following the important contractual phase of justification (where understanding of the Spirit's role has been dogged by self-contradictory proposals). I would suggest that these modern rereadings of Paul's soteriology allow for far greater focus on the Spirit, such that pneumatology is coherently integrated with the heart of Paul's understanding of God's gracious activity salvation. These matters can be explored in depth in Douglas Campbell's major work, *The Deliverance of God: An Apocalyptic Rereading of Justification in Paul*, for those brave enough to tackle such a massive tome.[7] But it will be a bravery well rewarded, for it is these exegetical developments, as they relate to the downfall of the contractual soteriology of justification theory, that will arguably lead to fresh engagement with New Testament pneumatology within the New Testament academic guild. More importantly, here are reasons why I have entitled this chapter 'Pneumatology and the New Testament' rather than 'New Testament Pneumatology', which I will explore later.

Though more could be said about contemporary New Testament academic concerns relating to pneumatology, just two more will be mentioned, and this will hopefully nicely balance the claims my colleague Lincoln Harvey has made with regards to the Spirit and the humanity of Jesus. Recent Pauline scholarship has begun to re-examine the relationship between New Testament

---

7 Douglas A. Campbell, The Deliverance of God: An Apocalyptic Rereading of Justification in Paul (Grand Rapids, MI: Eerdmans, 2009).

pneumatology and Christology in a way that can arguably pave the way for us to appreciate a very early Trinitarian-shaped faith, what one scholar has called a proto-Trinitarianism (see Gordon Fee's claims in his recent book *Pauline Christology*[8]). Certainly some scholars still sneer at this language, even those persuaded by an early divine-Christology, but a focus on early Christian pneumatology indeed demonstrates its appropriateness.

It is perhaps necessary to pause and explain the context of these debates. To what extent the earliest Christology can be called divine, that is, to what extent Christ can be put on the divine side of the line Jewish monotheism must draw between God and creatures in the very earliest church, continues to be debated. There are those who argue that a fully divine-Christology only comes later, in the Johannine writings, long after the historical Jesus, a Christology only hinted at in and indeed ultimately incompatible with Paul's theology (so Maurice Casey and, to a certain extent, Dunn). Against this, scholars like Larry Hurtado have argued that the divinity of Christ is evident from the way the early Christians included Christ in their corporate and cultic worship in a way that could only imply the full divinity of Christ. However, this has led to a sidelining of the Spirit, and so Hurtado asserts an early Christian binitarian pattern of worship, but not a Trinitarian one.

It is again Max Turner, and later his doctoral student, Mehrdad Fatehi, who provide food for thought. Based on the apostle's experience of the risen Christ and his lordship through the Spirit, Turner argues that:

Paul believes that the Spirit relates the presence and actions of the exalted Christ to the believer in ways that immediately

---

8 Gordon D. Fee, *Pauline Christology: An Exegetical-Theological Study* (Peabody: Hendrickson, 2007).

*evoke the analogy of the Spirit's extension of **God's** person and activity to humankind. It is difficult to see how such a claim would stop short of some form of 'divine' Christology.*[9]

Just as God's Spirit was God himself, present and active in the world, so Christ, in the same way, is present and active in the world through the Spirit. Christians confess that Christ is with them through the Spirit, evoking language Jews used to express the presence of God himself. Paul writes in Romans 15:18–19: 'For I will not venture to speak of anything except what Christ has accomplished through me to win obedience from the Gentiles, by word and deed, by the power of signs and wonders, by the power of the Spirit of God.' Or again, in 2 Corinthians 3:3, Paul explains that 'you show that you are a letter of Christ, prepared by us, written not with ink but with the Spirit of the living God, not on tablets of stone but on tablets of human hearts'. Christ works miracles and writes in hearts *through the Spirit*. All of this suggests, as Turner and Fatehi convincingly maintain, a divine Christology on the basis of a clear grasp of pneumatology; Christ's divinity is understood in relation to both Father and Spirit. It should not surprise us that experts of New Testament pneumatology are paving the way to a re-appreciation of the Trinitarian shaped faith of the first Christians.

Finally, one area of research could prove most fruitful in terms of early Christian pneumatology, namely the relationship between the covenantal promises associated with Abraham,

---

9   Max Turner, 'The Spirit of Christ and "Divine" Christology' in *Jesus of Nazareth: Lord and Christ. Essays on the Historical Jesus and New Testament Christology*, eds Joel B. Green and Max Turner (Carlisle: Paternoster, 1994), p. 434; bold his. Cf. also Max Turner, ' "Trinitarian" Pneumatology in the New Testament? – Towards an Explanation of the Worship of Jesus.' As *TJ* 58, no. 1 (2003): pp. 167–186; Mehrdad Fatehi, *The Spirit's Relation to the Risen Lord in Paul: An Examination of its Christological Implications*, WUNT II (Tübingen: Mohr, 2000).

particularly the inheritance of land, and Paul's understanding of the gift of the Spirit. So Paul writes in Galatians 3:13–14: 'Christ redeemed us from the curse of the law ... in order that in Christ Jesus the blessing of Abraham might come to the Gentiles, so that we might receive the promise of [... the land? No!] the Spirit through faith.' To what extent salvation-historical concerns, or the story of Israel, can or cannot clarify a text like this is a fascinating area of study.So much for some of the academic concerns regarding New Testament pneumatology. As has been pointed out above, New Testament pneumatology will mean different things to different readers.

Turning to a more popular audience, the concerns and range of questions differ considerably. In this context, the New Testament has often been employed, when brought into the orbit of pneumatology, to speak either for or against the contemporary ministry of the miraculous gifts of the Spirit listed in passages such as 1 Corinthians 12, Romans 12 and Ephesians 4. While it is tempting to brush over this debate, as it arguably has less to do with engagement with Scripture and more to do with certain modern Western worldview commitments (which is to say that the 'debate' is a little one-sided from an exegetical point of view), it remains of concern to many and so I will mention two key positions in the dispute.

On the one hand is the position of cessationism, which claims that the miraculous gifts of the Spirit were restricted to the apostolic age. Cessationism comes in 'hard' and 'soft' varieties, but space constraints don't permit discussion of the nuances. Miracles, cessationists tend to argue, are only seen in seasons of revelation, to confirm that message's entrance into the world. So Hebrews 2:3–4 states:

*how can we escape if we neglect so great a salvation? It was
declared at first through the Lord, and it was attested to us*

> *by those who heard him, while God added his testimony by*
> *signs and wonders and various miracles, and by gifts of the*
> *Holy Spirit, distributed according to his will.*

The end of New Testament revelation thus meant the end of
miracles. With the final full-stop of the New Testament there
was no longer any need to confirm the new message. So Paul
wrote in 1 Corinthians 13:

> *Love never ends. But as for prophecies, they will come to an*
> *end; as for tongues, they will cease; as for knowledge, it will*
> *come to an end. For we know only in part, and we prophesy*
> *only in part; but when the complete comes, the partial will*
> *come to an end. When I was a child, I spoke like a child, I*
> *thought like a child, I reasoned like a child; when I became*
> *an adult, I put an end to childish ways. For now we see in a*
> *mirror, dimly, but then we will see face to face.*

On the other hand, New Testament scholars will tend to find
these cessationist arguments either bizarre or hopelessly
question – begging, misconstruing the nature of New Testament
revelation as well as the import of Pauline texts such as the one
just quoted, which, I should add, refers not to the closing of the
canon but to the final, eschatological unveiling of Jesus Christ,
when all will finally see (presumably Christ) face to face. More
positively, the New Testament generally seems to propose that
the gifts of the Spirit continue in the 'last days'. So Acts 2:16–
17 cites from Joel: 'this is what was spoken through the prophet
Joel: "in the last days it will be, God declares, that I will pour
out my Spirit upon all flesh, and your sons and your daughters
shall prophesy, and your young men shall see visions, and your
old men shall dream dreams."' Noteworthy is that these last days
are understood to have begun with Jesus and his first disciples,

so Hebrews 1:2 states: 'but in these last days he has spoken to us by a Son'. Likewise Paul speaks, in 1 Corinthians 10:11, of his readers and himself, as 'us, on whom the ends of the ages have come' etc. The claims of the Johannine Jesus concur: 'Very truly, I tell you, the one who believes in me will also do the works that I do and, in fact, will do greater works than these, because I am going to the Father' (John 14:12). Much more could be said here, but this is at least a flavour of the debate.

Perhaps a more evenly balanced topic of debate concerns the contemporary discussion about whether the spiritual gift of 'tongues', which Paul discusses in 1 Corinthians 12–14, is to be understood as an ability to speak another *human* language (as it appears to be in Acts), or whether Paul meant a *non-human* (angelic?) language, thus something compatible with the expression of tongues found in contemporary charismatic worship.

In terms of those concerned about traditional theological propositions, New Testament pneumatology is again read differently, such that debate has arisen regarding the distinguishable personhood and divinity of the Holy Spirit in the New Testament. This is understandable, for it is, of course, more than just desirable for Christians to be able to claim a strong New Testament basis for orthodox theological affirmations regarding the Trinity! In this regard it is typical to focus engagement with texts where the Spirit seems to be characterised in personal ways, that he (or it? or she?) can be grieved, that he teaches, searches, intercedes, and so on. Most biblical scholars will indeed confirm that the Spirit of God, in the Bible, is best understood as *God himself* as he interacts with and relates to the world. The extent to which the personhood of the thus divine Spirit can be distinguished from the Father and the Son requires further interaction with the New Testament, especially parts of John's Gospel, where the Spirit is spoken of as *another paraclētos*, which can be variously translated as counsellor, comforter, helper, or perhaps best, Advocate. So the Johannine Jesus prays: 'I will ask the Father, and he will give you another Advocate, to be with you forever' (14:16). From verses such as these the divine personal Spirit can thus be distinguished from both Father and Son, and once difficult verses such as 2 Corinthians 3:17 are carefully negotiated, an orthodox Trinitarianism can at least be scripturally supported.

Of course, this handling of pneumatology, with respect to the New Testament, does not go unchallenged, at both exegetical and hermeneutical levels. So some will respond that this is unwarrantedly to import much later and alien dogmatic categories back on to New Testament texts. However, while there is legitimacy to these concerns, it must not be forgotten that dogmatics and exegesis do not exist in separate realms (despite the influential distinctions of eighteenth- and ninteenth-century German scholarship – eg Johann Gabler). The subject matter of these New Testament texts is theological – they concern God – and the very process of the canonical selection of these texts involved dogmatic categories.[10] To pose orthodox dogmatic questions to the text is thus not illegitimate. As a New Testament specialist, I would simply stress that those who use the New Testament in this way remain hermeneutically self aware, ie to recognise that such issues may be asking texts to answer questions that those texts were not necessarily penned to answer directly.

---

10 Craig D. Allert, *A High View of Scripture?: The Authority of the Bible and the Formation of the New Testament Canon* (Grand Rapids, MI: Baker Academic, 2007).

PNEUMATOLOGY FOR THE NEW TESTAMENT

So much for contemporary concerns relating the New Testament and pneumatology. I offer two final thoughts and two final reasons why this chapter has been entitled 'Pneumatology and the New Testament' and not 'New Testament pneumatology'.

Biblical scholars, who have devoted much time and attention to pneumatology, provide a service for all biblical scholarship in perhaps more ways than they know. A great gulf has, in academic theology, been forged between the world and language of systematic theology, on the one hand, and biblical studies on the other (here I must throw another critical glance at Gabler). Can this gulf be crossed, or, even, should it be? Enter pneumatology.

Late nineteenth-century biblical scholarship domesticated even spirit language to accord to the German tradition of Idealism, so that spirit concerned 'the moral sphere of human attainment' (Levison[11]), or the 'Principle of the Christian Consciousness' (F. C. Baur[12]). In this context New Testament pneumatology could be kept safely domesticated within the world of historical study, away from religious enthusiasts. Yet in 1888, Hermann Gunkel burst into this scene to remind scholarship that the Spirit, in early Christian thought, has less to do with abstract idealism and more to do with the 'mysterious and overwhelming in human life' (Gunkel[13]). His voice should echo down the twentieth century and into the twenty-first, for too often New Testament scholarship pretends that its subject matter is the containable, the measurable or the quantifiable. But pneumatology reminds New Testament readers that its subject matter concerns *God*, and not merely the God of the philosophers, or the deist God of

---

11 John R. Levison, *Filled with the Spirit*, p. 3
12 *op. cit.*, p. 4.
13 *op. cit.*, p. 3.

the Enlightenment, but rather the living and active God, who, to use theological jargon for a moment, keeps popping up to do and inspire stuff in ways that tend to embarrass the polite, the safe and the bourgeois.

It is perhaps not a surprise, then, to discover that one of the leading proponents of a theological reading of the New Testament, one which aims to re-engage dialogue between the worlds of systematic theology and biblical study, is none other than one of the world's leading New Testament experts on the Holy Spirit, Max Turner. Pneumatology reminds the New Testament scholar that the God in the pages of this set of historical documents, truly to be examined with all historical-critical rigour, is the *living God*, the present and active Lord. Hence to state that New Testament studies need pneumatology is not simply to state the obvious, that the Spirit can work in and through biblical scholarship, but that the living God, as powerful and active by his Spirit, stands as a corrective to a scholarship solely concerned with the academic and, in not just some cases, the irrelevant. God, by his Spirit, keeps popping up, shaking categories and peering though historical-critical ruminations to lovingly disturb – even the world of New Testament scholarship.

A final reason to speak about 'pneumatology and the New Testament', and not 'New Testament Pneumatology': let us remember the relational dynamic involved in much modern systematic theological proposals. Moltmann has written that the 'New Testament talks about God by proclaiming in narrative the relationships of the Father, the Son and the Spirit, which are relationships of fellowship and are *open to the world*'.[14] Elsewhere he writes of the significance of 'partnership, a

---

14 Jürgen Moltmann, *The Trinity and the Kingdom: The Doctrine of God* (Minneapolis: Fortress, 1981), p. 64, italics mine.

mutual relationship, even about friendship between God and free man', and that '[w]ithout the social relation there can be no personality'.[15] Grenz speaks of the 'near consensus that *person* is a relational concept',[16] Lash, admittedly perhaps problematically, claims, God *is* the relations he has,[17] Zizioulas states that 'without the concept of communion it would not be possible to speak of the being of God',[18] and LaCugna opines, 'God's way of being in relationship *with us* – which is God's personhood – is a perfect expression of God's being as God.'[19] To this list of theologians, one could add many more, such as some of the Torrances, LeRon Shults, and even Karl Barth (and this is not to even mention the many important figures in older church history, such as the Cappadocian Fathers). But the New Testament expert is often at a loss to know how to handle such claims; these theologians, it seems, do indeed speak a different language from the biblical scholar trained with various critical methodological Bible reading tools! But as has been pointed out above, a New Testament affirmation of divine-Christology, one which includes Christ on the divine side of the line monotheism must draw between God and creatures, should necessarily deal with New Testament pneumatology and the relationality of God. The New Testament link between pneumatology and divine-Christology should thus facilitate the New Testament expert to

---

15 Moltmann, *Trinity*, pp.144–145. Furthermore, not only are social scientists and psychotherapists increasingly understanding the 'self' as 'constituted in and through relationships' (Shults, F. LeRon, and Steven J. Sandage. *Transforming Spirituality: Integrating Theology and Psychology* (Grand Rapids: Baker, 2006), p. 25; but such language finds even more enthusiastic employment as these disciplines engage with theology (Shults and Sandage, *Transforming*, cf. 161–166, 221–233).

16 Stanley J. Grenz, *The Social God and the Relational Self: A Trinitarian Theology of the Imago Dei* (Louisville: Westminster John Knox, 2001), p. 9, italics his.

17 Cf. Nicholas Lash, *Believing Three Ways in One God : A Reading of the Apostles' creed* (London : Notre Dame Press, 1993).

18 J. D. Zizioulas, *Being as Communion: Studies in Personhood and the Church* (Crestwood, NY: St Vladimir's Seminary Press, 1985), p. 17.

19 Catherine M. LaCugna, *God for Us : The Trinity and Christian Life* (New York: Harper Sanfrancisco, 1991), pp. 304 –305, italics hers..

re-engage such claims via the New Testament's Christological discourse, and thus reopen dialogue not only between those two unhappily divided worlds, that of the systematic theologian and biblical scholar, but also between the New Testament scholar and the church, where Christ, *by his Spirit*, is present and active.[20]

---

20 For more on this parting thought, cf. the final appendix in Chris Tilling, '*Paul's Divine-Christology: The Relation Between the Risen Lord and Believers in Paul, and the Divine-Christology Debate'* (Brunel University: PhD thesis, 2009).

11 A BIBLE STUDY OF MATTHEW 12:22–32

JANE WILLIAMS

This passage is exegetically, theologically and pastorally difficult, so it seems important to address it, even if it is not, at first sight, an obvious place from which to start to celebrate the Holy Spirit.

The Holy Spirit often appears in our theology and practice as the 'cuddly' member of the Trinity, primarily concerned with the creation and maintenance of relationship. Augustine famously called the Holy Spirit 'the bond of love', and Paul's letters see the gifts of the Spirit as given to build up the community of Christians. Yet the passage we are exploring today says that the only unforgivable sin is the sin against the Holy Spirit. How can these two things be reconciled?

The passage is found in both Matthew and Mark, with a slightly different setting in each case. In Mark (3:20–30), Jesus' family are questioning his sanity, and are enthusiastically backed up by the 'scribes', who want to suggest that Jesus' power comes from a demonic source. In Matthew, the exchange is set firmly in the context of conflict between Jesus and the religious authorities of the day. Matthew says explicitly that Jesus has healed a demoniac, and that the accusation has been made that only demons can have power over demons. Luke (11:14–23) records the exchange about the source of Jesus' power, and the suggestion that it has evil roots, but he does not repeat the saying about the sin against the Holy Spirit. But all three agree that Jesus vigorously defends himself, saying that evil does not fight against evil.

The saying seems to be at its strongest in Matthew. Jesus protests, emphatically, that his miracles are performed through God's power, and that that can only mean that 'the kingdom of God has come'. Matthew usually avoids saying 'the kingdom of God', preferring to speak of the 'kingdom of heaven', which would be a phrase much more acceptable to Jewish audiences, where the name of God is treated with the reticence of awe. The words bring out the forcefulness of Jesus' response, and make it clear how much this exchange matters.

There is no agreement among commentators on this passage about what the unforgivable sin of 'speaking against the Holy Spirit' means, and many Christians have worried themselves into terror, fearing that they might have committed this dreadful sin.

So to come to the pastoral reverberations of this passage first of all: this is not something that can be done by accident. In J. K. Rowling's final Harry Potter book, *The Deathly Hallows*, Voldemort, the powerful, evil wizard is trying to find Harry and his friends, who are on the run. He sets up an ingenious piece of magic, which instantly draws attention to anyone who says the name 'Voldemort'. He knows that most people are too terrified ever to speak the name, so that anyone brave enough or foolhardy enough to do so is likely to be an enemy. The trap works. Harry and his friends use the dreaded name as a symbol that they cannot be controlled by its bearer, and they are caught. I've already given away a vital twist in the plot, so I won't go on. But the point is that speaking against the Holy Spirit is not like this. It is not a cruel game or a trap. God is not waiting to pounce on anyone who unwittingly misuses the powerful name. If you are afraid that you may have committed this sin, then let me reassure you – you haven't. The very fact that you are anxious about it shows you haven't done it. I repeat: it cannot be done by accident.

In its context, here in Matthew's Gospel, it looks as though what is being described is a cold, clear-eyed determination not to distinguish between good and evil, but only between what suits me and what doesn't. It looks like a willingness to see the power that liberates another as bad, if I do not benefit from it. Someone else's flourishing is not in my interest, and so the one who brings about that flourishing is evil. No other moral measure is acknowledged: only my own well-being.

So the people who are suggesting that Jesus' miracles are done through the use of demonic power have decided that they will not be convinced. Ideally, they would like to be able to deny that any healing had taken place at all, but the crowd will not accept that; the evidence is too strong. So, failing that, they need to undermine the miracle-worker. What Jesus is doing does not suit them: it calls into question their own status, religious, political, cultural and personal, and so it is not good. They have no interest in how the healed person sees it, or the hope it brings to the others crowding around Jesus, the hope that God is near, that God cares, that God reaches out to the worthless, the suffering, the unimportant. None of that matters to the ones questioning Jesus. None of it counts as a means of assessing where Jesus' power comes from.

It isn't even clear from the passage that the scoffers believe their own analysis. Perhaps they do. But perhaps they just do not care. Perhaps the question of whether this really is the presence and power of the goodness of God is a minor matter to them, because wherever the power comes from, they are not benefiting from it or controlling it.

So, in this context, to 'speak against the Holy Spirit' is to speak with a calculated determination to expunge what is of no benefit to us personally, and to sneer at even the greatest goodness, if it doesn't profit us. It is a deliberate rejection of any measure of morality apart from self-interest. If it is not good for me, it is not good, full stop.

And actually, this is surprisingly rare in our world. Major emergencies and natural disasters call out spontaneous empathy and generosity, over and over again. Reports of the mistreatment of children horrify us. Over and over again, we demonstrate that we can tell the difference between good and evil, even when we are not involved. Over and over again, we show that we know something, instinctively, about our common humanity, so that the suffering of another matters to us, even when there is no obvious motive of self-interest.

This passage in Matthew connects, perhaps, to John 16:7–11, where Jesus promises us that the Holy Spirit, the advocate, institutes a new way of judging. The Holy Spirit reminds us that, actually, the world is not arranged for our comfort, and it is not amenable to our preferred way of working. The world is created for the flourishing, redemption and renewal of all creation in Christ Jesus. Those who condemned Jesus to death had forgotten that. They had taught themselves to believe that they, not God, made the rules. They had taught themselves to imagine that their judgement was final. And, in that sense, they had broken the first commandment, to put nothing in the place of God. Almost without noticing, they had put themselves, their needs, their judgements, in the place of God.

In Matthew's Gospel, the people who question Jesus want to believe that good is evil so that they do not have to change. In all the Gospels, this human determination to set ourselves up as judges of the world is what leads to the crucifixion. The human judgement on Jesus is shown up for what it is when God raises Jesus from the dead. No wonder John says that we need the Holy Spirit to reset our judgements about the world!

But if *judgement* is one of the traits associated with the Holy Spirit, why is that good news, and how can we receive and exercise this spiritual gift?

Christians have sometimes chosen to act as though the discernment of the Holy Spirit is a personal gift, given to us to exercise. It gives us a right to judge others, or to tell others what to do, because the Holy Spirit is our personal hotline to the will of God. So the primary purpose of the judgement of the Holy Spirit is to make us feel superior and to ensure that we are always in the right. This seems a bit of a waste of the magisterial power that John 16 is referring to. It's a bit as though we assume that the whole power of the National Grid is set up to allow us to run our nose-hair clippers. There is the nation crying out for electricity, but we are diverting it all to our cosmetic needs. There is the universe desperate for the wisdom of the Spirit, and we are confining it to the amount we want.

But the Holy Spirit works to give us the discernment to see Jesus, and so to know the reality of the world. To see Jesus is to know God as our Father, and the Spirit as the one who draws us into God's creative project for the transformation of all that is. Nothing less.

When God comes to reveal himself and save the world, it is Jesus we see; when the Holy Spirit comes in power, to lead us into all truth, it is so that we can witness to Jesus. When God comes to judge the world, we will recognise our judge in the human face of Jesus. To exercise the gifts of the Spirit is to look for Jesus and, when we find him, to help others to see him, too. As we look for the work of the Holy Spirit in the world, we are looking for the pattern of Jesus. We are looking for signs of self-

_ .ving love, of people working for human flourishing, reaching out across barriers, liberating, healing, forgiving; in these activities we recognise the shape of Jesus' own ministry among us. We are also looking for the pattern of the cross: for those condemned unjustly, for those despised and outcast, for those who suffer, for those whom the world judges to be worthless, expendable. Our Spirit-inspired sensors will quiver with the expectation of encountering Jesus, there where he freely chose to go: on the cross.

And when we see the shape of Jesus, in whatever unlikely places, how will we respond? How will the Spirit's gift of discernment work in us? I would like to suggest that it will make us a people of praise. 'Orthodoxy' is often translated as 'correct doctrine', but it really means 'correct praise'. We who know how to praise God in all his works are 'orthodox'. Wherever we see, with the help of the Holy Spirit, the hint, the glimpse, the shadow, the whisper of Jesus, we give thanks and praise, and we set to work to excavate the shape, to build on it, to bring it to light, to join in with it, to make it visible to all around, because that is what the Holy Spirit is doing.

The power of the Holy Spirit will help us to see the shape of Jesus, the seeds of Jesus, where, whether they know it or not, people are working to remake humanity in the image of God. And we will praise the Lord wherever we find him. Remaking the world in the image of Jesus is not confined to the church; politicians may do it, bankers may do it, teachers, doctors and nurses, unemployed people, suffering people, dying people. But we Christians, exercising the discernment of the Holy Spirit, can see it and praise it. We thank God for it, but we can also thank those who may not even know that they are helping the world to see the love of God in Jesus Christ.

The eighteenth-century poet, Christopher Smart, wrote a poem ('Jubilate Agno') in praise of his cat, part of a longer poem praising the lamb of God. Smart writes:

> *For I will consider my Cat Jeoffry.*
> *For he is the servant of the Living God, duly and daily*
> *serving him.*
> *For at the first glance of the glory of God in the East he*
> *worships in his way.*
> *For is this done by wreathing his body seven times round*
> *with elegant quickness.*
> *For then he leaps up to catch the musk, which is the blessing*
> *of God upon his prayer ...*
> *For he keeps the Lord's watch in the night against the*
> *adversary.*
> *For he counteracts the powers of darkness by his electrical*
> *skin and glaring eyes.*
> *For he counteracts the Devil, who is death, by brisking*
> *about the life.*[1]

We probably do not need to analyse the theology of this poem in too much depth, or necessarily agree with it, but its attitude is surely right. The poet sees the beauty and vitality of his much-loved cat as a gift from and to God, and he gives thanks and praise. Those are the eyes we need as we see God's world. We are looking for the ways in which all things duly and daily serve God, in their own way.

So if the work of the Holy Spirit in the world is to show Jesus, then those who receive the gifts of the Spirit are privileged to discern Jesus-like patterns, wherever they are found. 'It is our duty and our joy at all times and in all places to give God thanks and praise', as the Prayer Book says. Our thanks and our praise

---

1 This poem can be found in many collections, or at http://42opus.com/v4n2/mycatjeoffry

are far more constructive ways of making Jesus visible than our blame and our anger. Each disciple of Christ is here not because God has angrily blamed us for our sins, but because God in Christ has reached out to us in love, to lead us away from sin and death through the power of light and love. 'Ransomed, healed, restored, forgiven, who like us his praise should sing?'

Praise is a powerful agent of transformation – any parent or teacher will tell you that. It is the opposite of the sin against the Holy Spirit, which cannot bear any goodness that does not serve its own selfish ends. Those who receive the gift of the Holy Spirit are enabled to praise God, and to share that praise with a world that longs to know that it is worthy of praise. When we ask for the power of the Spirit, we are asking for this great gift of praise and discernment, to enable us to see goodness, however weak, or hidden, or unsure of itself, and to celebrate it into greater life. All that is of God finds its source and goal in Jesus Christ. As the Holy Spirit draws all things towards their true life, let us sing the Spirit's glad hymn of praise, 'Make a joyful noise to God, all the earth!' (Psalm 66:1).

12 REFLECTION: MOTIFS IN THE THEOLOGY OF THE HOLY SPIRIT IN THE WORLD TODAY CONFERENCE

TOM GREGGS

It is timely and significant that this book (and the conference at which these papers were first presented) has engaged in an in-depth consideration of the doctrine of the Holy Spirit. Karl Barth, the theological mountain through which it seems almost inevitable that theologians must tunnel – or over which they must pass – stated towards the end of his life that he dreamed of a future theology that was not viewed, as his own had been, from the dominant perspective of Christology but primarily from the perspective of pneumatology.[1]

In a world in which Pentecostalism is the fastest growing ecclesial movement, and in which charismatic worship has become a pervasive trans-denominational means of expressing the intensity of Christian faith, Barth's own theological desire for successive theological generations is a pressing need and

---

1 Eberhard Busch, *Karl Barth: His Life from Letters and Autobiographical Texts*, trans. John Bowden (London: SCM, 1976), p. 494.

requirement for a world church that is clearly being touched today by fresh and new outpourings of God's Holy Spirit. If theology is at all concerned to support the church in thinking about and seeking to articulate what it means to believe in God, Father, Son *and Holy Spirit*, then to attend especially in the present ecclesial and theological season to the doctrine of the Holy Spirit is surely a wise and necessary service that theology can perform.

In that way, it is fundamentally appropriate that this book has been formed with due attention to both church and academy, and that the lectures, talks, sermons and 'GodPods', have recognised the innate relationship between church proclamation and teaching, and theological reflection on that teaching. To a degree, the agenda for theology has been set by reawakenings, not only (positively) to the Holy Spirit's dynamic and intensive work through the charismatic and Pentecostal movements, but also (negatively) to some form of generalised or New Age spirituality that is all too evident in our culture and (while there are dangers in the use of this term) in the post-modern 'pick and mix' approach to matters relating to God: any trip to a high street book shop makes plain the shift from 'theology' (now a non-existent general bookshop category) to 'spirituality' (in all of its weird and wonderful forms).

It is commendable therefore that the 2010 conference on The Holy Spirit in the World Today has asked the academy to step up to the mark to help to equip the church with theological reflection on the doctrine of the Holy Spirit, and that the academics involved have reflected theologically on issues that relate to lived ecclesial life and to the life of faith in the twenty-first century. Too often, two dialogues have tended to take place in theology – one dialogue between those who speak from lecterns in lecture theatres and another dialogue between those who speak in pulpits or work in churches. By attending to only one of these contexts, fundamental theological material will be lost on both sides. The conference held at Holy Trinity Brompton in London brought together church ministry and theological reflection in a way that is much needed, but (in the UK at least) often painfully rare. We were blessed at this conference by this wise and fruitful combination.

But there is also a *theological* reason for the importance of the church and academy joining together to consider pneumatology. The Spirit is not only the one who founds the church at Pentecost (Acts 2) and in Christ's breathing the Spirit onto the disciples (John 20:21–23), but the Spirit is also the one who leads us into *all truth* (John 16:13). At best, academic theology should imagine itself as an exercise born of reflection upon the Spirit of God in leading human beings into all truth.[2] This truth does not simply involve some form of theoretical assent to a cognitive act. Truth in Scripture (*aletheia*) involves the whole of the person; it is truth in the sense of 'reality' more than singularly theoretical speculation. The dynamic operation of the Spirit in leading us into all truth, all reality, involves, therefore, both the process of being led into the ever-deeper reality of God's living presence found within the life of the church, *and* being led into the reality of life as created beings within the world to which the Spirit ministers.

Thus, for example, Professor Volf's discussion of globalisation and religious diversity, presented at the conference (and found in Chapter 2 of this volume), is immensely important, and reflects profoundly on the need to engage in theology simultaneously from the perspective of church and university.

---

2   On the theme of the breadth of theological reflection, see Daniel W. Hardy, 'Creation and Eschatology', in *The Doctrine of Creation: Essays in Dogmatics, History and Philosophy*, ed. Colin E. Gunton (London & New York; T & T Clark, 2004), pp. 105–133; cf. Wolfhart Pannenberg *Systematic Theology Vol. 2* (Edinburgh: T&T Clark, 1994), pp. 61ff.

Both the lives of the church and of the academy, as places in which truth is sought, are places in which the work of the Holy Spirit of God who leads us into *all* truth is operative. And it is here, perhaps, where Professor David Ford's reflections on wisdom (a gift of the Holy Spirit) are deeply resonant with the whole foundational idea of this conference.[3] In short, we might say that the idea of the conference itself was the fruit of a deeply pneumatological manner of thinking: it was not simply a conference on pneumatology but a conference whose very conception embodied a pneumatological logic and dynamic.

But what might be said of the pneumatological teachings that this conference and book have offered to us? Here, I am conscious of being able only to offer motifs and trends, without any suggestion that these might be synthesising or unifying principles that bind the papers of the conference together. While these motifs are no doubt superfluous, it is hoped that they may help us to digest some of the wisdom that the conference has offered to us. In identifying these trends and motifs, I hope that I might be forgiven for not simply repeating inadequately and descriptively the words that the other chapters of this book have so eloquently offered us already. Instead, I wish to offer some overarching thoughts and reflections on the pneumatology that the conference offered us.

PNEUMATOLOGY IS AN ENGAGEMENT IN THEOLOGY FROM THE MIDDLE

One point by which I was continually struck throughout the conference was that pneumatology is an engagement in theology *from the middle*. Attending to pneumatology involves attending

---

3   For further detailed discussion of Ford on wisdom, see David F. Ford, *Christian Wisdom: Desiring God and Learning in Love* (Cambridge: CUP, 2007). See also Chapter 3 of this book.

to the third article of the creed, attending to *the things of the Spirit (or the economy of the Spirit) as well as to the person of the Spirit*. Jürgen Moltmann discussed the work of the Spirit in the church; others looked at ethics and ecclesiology in relation to pneumatology. But the conference also, importantly, contained worship and a sermon by the present Archbishop of Canterbury. Within the more academic reflection, moreover, biography and autobiography were frequently deployed, attesting to the work of the Spirit in the lives of real people and churches through lectures, testimony and interviews.

Since it is the doctrine that attends to the work of the Spirit, pneumatology must always, therefore, attend to the church, the communion of saints, the forgiveness of sins, redemption, and so on. Thus, attending to pneumatology involves attending to the complexity and the excitement of living faithful lives of discipleship in the present world in which we live. And this instantly begins to open up falsely drawn boundaries and binaries to which the church and theology are susceptible. Focusing on pneumatology determines that we focus on God's present work in creation, in continuity with God's narrative known to us in Jesus Christ. Considering the work of the Holy Spirit involves, not only asking questions about God's self-revelation, but also asking questions of the way in which we might know and receive that revelation now; not only asking questions about God's work of salvation, but also asking questions of the effects of that work of salvation in the church and the world of which we are a part; not only considering God's creative activity, but also considering God's contingent contemporaneity (God's here and nowness) with creation today; not only being reminded of the future redemption of creation, but also being reminded of the present forgiveness of sins and the sanctified life.

In a sense, all theology involves beginning with the Holy Spirit, since it is by the Spirit that we may proclaim Jesus as Lord (1 Corinthians 12:3), and are able subjectively to know anything of God at all. But focusing particularly on pneumatology forces theology to recognise that it engages in an activity from the middle – from the perspective of the here and now for those to whom the pledge and guarantee of salvation has been given; from the viewpoint of those still present within creation and anticipating the future return of Christ; from the recognition of human involvement in the reception of God's message of salvation, and the help of God in our responding to his salvific work.

Focusing on pneumatology focuses the church on the present, on the world, and on the God who is present to the world, but it does so always with an eye to the knowledge of the future redemption to which creation is oriented. Pneumatology asks theology to recognise that it can never simply start with God alone or humanity alone in its presentation of the message of the Christian faith; and it reminds theology (to employ a dreadful and corny phrase) that it must begin with where people are at – not because people are there (though that helps!) but because God is present there in the person of his Holy Spirit.

THE DOCTRINE BY WHICH WE ENGAGE MOST FULLY WITH THE CHURCH

Related to my first point, pneumatology is a doctrine that offers a reminder to theology of the ecclesial nature of its discourse. This point is raised throughout this book, not least in Jürgen Moltmann's discussions of 'The Church in the Power of the Spirit', which challenges us to think and act locally, and which begins with discussions of his own particularities and communities. His words about participatory community and his focus on the gifts of the Spirit reminded me – as a Methodist – of Wesley, not only of his focus on the local class, but also his words about the gifts of the Spirit – that God 'fits us for whatever he calls us to'.[4]

Of all of the doctrinal loci, pneumatology is the one that is most bound up with the life of the church, since – after all – the Spirit is the one who creates, sustains and sanctifies the people of God. It is highly appropriate, therefore, that in considering the work of the Holy Spirit, we should consider the operations of the Spirit in the life of the empirical church; and indeed that in this context we should worship and we should pray. Of all of the doctrines, the doctrine of the Holy Spirit is the one that is surely least forgiving if the experience of faith is not directly discussed, since it is, we should not forget, the Spirit by whom we experience God. Discussions of the church allow us to see the operative dynamics of the Spirit within the lives of the people of God, and also to recognise something of the Spirit's unpredictability and (even) wildness: the Spirit is, after all, pictured as the one who blows wherever he chooses. Attending to Pentecostal and charismatic expressions of faith, as well as to the still small voice of calm that the Spirit brings in an equally powerful and tangential way, to the work of the Spirit in convicting the world of sin, and to the leading of the Spirit in the life of discipleship is fitting, if we are to do any justice at all to the reality of the life of the Spirit in the church and the lives of the saints – the data on which theology reflects.[5]

---

4 John Wesley, 'On Redeeming the Time', *The Works of John Welsey 1872 Edition*, (Grand Rapids, MI: Baker, 1979), Sermon 93.6.

5 I am taking for granted that the doctrine of the Spirit is directly connected to the life of the church. This contrasts to more 'culture-based' pneumatologies which identify the Spirit with Hegelian *Geist* and with the Spirit of the age: see, for example, Paul Tillich, *Systematic Theology Vol. 3: Life in the Spirit; History and the Kingdom of God* (Welwyn: James Nisbet & Co., 1964); and Peter Hodgson, *Winds of the Spirit* (London: SCM, 1994). Such pneumatologies build upon the biblical imagery associated with the Spirit in the likes of Genesis 1 (in which the Spirit moves over the waters) and Psalm 139 (in which the Spirit is inescapable), but often arise out of a confusion of the Holy Spirit with the spirit of life that is used to describe human existence as a gift from God in the Old Testament (eg Genesis 6:3). One might even detect elements of this kind

However, we cannot simply reduce pneumatology to ecclesiology. Ecclesiology is always a *subset* of pneumatology, and not the other way around. Put formally, one might say that the presence of the Spirit is the *sine qua non* of the church, but the church is not the *sine qua non* of the presence of the Spirit, who in freedom blows wherever he wills (John 3:8). Ordering the doctrines appropriately helps us to recognise this. It is thus only as an act of the Spirit that the church is brought into being in time, but the acts of the Spirit are not simply the bringing into being of the *ecclesia* in history. God is the God who 'sets our feet on a broad place'. Moltmann reminds us that there are clear implications for the world, which arise from the church that lives in the life of the Spirit.

THE CONTEMPORANEITY AND FUTURITY OF THE SPIRIT

Another important concern, I think, which has come through in these papers is the relationship between the 'nowness' and the 'futureness' of the Spirit. Archbishop Rowan Williams, in Chapter 4, speaks of hope as 'earnest, energetic yearning and longing'. And Professor Moltmann points us to our call to pray '*Marantha*', and to live in the hope of the reconciliation of the whole cosmos.

The contemporaneity and futureness of the work of the Spirit is a way in which we can account for the intensities of faith in a world of ambiguity, the desire we have for the unreachable God. It is the manner by which we might live as Christians without replacing the kingdom of God in our minds with the

---

of approach in the very thorough book by Michael Welker, *God the Spirit*, trans. John F. Hoffmeyer (Minneapolis: Fortress Press, 1994). My own approach seeks to follow creedal patterns, and to focus appropriately on the *holiness* of the Holy Spirit (see p. 184ff.).

desire for a present and personally conceived utopia, but also without giving up on the fact that God's will is breaking into the world by the activity of the church and people of faith. The gift of the Holy Spirit between the ascension and the return of Christ demonstrates that the present is important; that we should not simply be people focused away from the world, but should be a people focused on the world: after all, Jesus tells us that it is better that he goes away, since he is sending another counsellor (John 16:7). Archbishop Williams reminds us of the connection between the Spirit in the world today and the real co-humanity that the Spirit creates, a theme further brought out profoundly and deeply in Miroslav Volf's words. But the Spirit also reminds us that the world is being redeemed, and that what we have presently is a *pledge* or *guarantee* of future salvation.

The Spirit is the one, therefore, who realises (or begins to realise) the event of salvation in the present. Through the Spirit, salvation becomes not only something which takes place behind us in Christ and ahead of us in the *eschaton*, but also something that is real in the present through the Spirit, who is ever present in and to the believer between those two events.

This is striking within the biblical account: in Paul, it is the Spirit who provides the guarantee of future salvation in the present (2 Corinthians 5:5 and Ephesians 1:3–4).[6] The effect of this, moreover, is significant in altering the present: the pledge and guarantee of our salvation does not involve merely a waiting in anticipation of something which lies in the future; it does not involve a simple piece of knowledge that we store away; but it involves present *transformation*.

---

6 Cf. Colin Gunton, 'Atonement and the Triune God', in *Theology after Liberalism: A Reader*, ed. John Webster and George Schner (Oxford: Blackwell Publishers, 2000), p. 128: 'the Spirit is God enabling the world to be itself, to realise its eschatological perfection'.

This can be seen in Paul's discussion of the fruits of the Holy Spirit, in which the person who is filled with and guided by the Holy Spirit knows God's salvation in Jesus Christ, and is, therefore, freed to be able to be loving, joyous, patient, kind, generous, faithful, gentle and self-controlled (Galatians 5:22–25). Knowledge of the ultimate future with God in Christ through the indwelling of the Holy Spirit in the present alters the person's life in the present: the Spirit begins to realise the promise of salvation now through the future guarantee that is offered.

As Miroslav Volf puts it, the Spirit allows humans to flourish. Or, in Rowan Williams's words, the Spirit causes a 'yearning to become what we were made for'; a yearning to be present with Jesus in calling God 'Abba'; a yearning to be with Christ and to grow by the Spirit towards being God's child, and thus to become fully human by participating in Christ's self-offering.

THE HOLINESS OF THE SPIRIT

The idea of the present work of the Spirit in the church and in the world determines that there is a need to consider what one might offer as the conditions by which to recognise the operations of the Spirit. There is always a danger that pneumatology all too easily draws lines uncritically from culture to God, identifying God's Spirit as present in any and every *Zeitgeist*. There is a danger, put simply, that we reduce the Holy Spirit to some sort of 'slushy' human spirituality.[7] When we consider the Spirit,

---

7 'Most people who use religious language at all use "spirit" as the opposite of "matter": for them, the word denotes, in the vaguest and most general way, whatever transcends the material or belongs to "the other world". "A spirit" might mean a spectre or a ghost (and "ghost" is etymologically akin to *Geist*, the German word for "spirit"). The Bible, however, for the most part uses the words rendered by "spirit" in a more restricted and more specialized way.' C. F. D. Moule, *The Holy Spirit* (London & New York: Continuum, 2000), p. 1.

therefore, it is important always to lay appropriate stress on the *holiness* of the Holy Spirit. This holiness that Scripture demonstrates to as sometimes strange and unexpected, and we should surely expect nothing different from the Spirit who blows wherever he wills.

But it is also a holiness that we have seen embodied in the one on whom the Spirit rested most fully – Jesus Christ. We do well to remember the concern never to separate Word and Spirit, and to see the identifying presence of the Spirit as that which makes creation more Christlike. It has been good to hear something of the interrelation of the work of Christ and of the Spirit at this conference: we cannot think of these as two works, after all, and we must remember that in any act of the Godhead, all members of the Trinity are present.

Again, this theme of the Spirit's holiness has been touched upon variously in the papers contained in this book. However, I am struck by the fact that the holiness of the Holy Spirit is such that the effect of the Spirit's presence might not always be one which immediately feels positive, or warm and 'fuzzy': we may find ourselves, like Peter in the boat with Jesus (Luke 5:8), or Isaiah in the temple (Isaiah 6:5), somehow wishing to escape from the reality of God's presence. As Archbishop Williams puts it, realising what we've signed up to should bring about the experience of saying to God, 'Stop it!'. While pneumatology may well be a way that we might speak of God's actions in work and culture, outside the walls of the church, the presence of the Spirit might not always be about affirming the world or culture; the Spirit's holiness means it might well be likely that we hear him utter a 'no' (cf. John 16:8–11) – a 'no' directed towards ourselves on whom he rests most intensely, rather than to be directed by us rather morally and superiorly to others.[8]

---

8 For further explorations of this theme, see Simeon Zahl, 'Reformation Pessimism

Attention to the Spirit requires the need always to remember the holiness of the Spirit.

THE INTENSITY AND EXTENSITY OF THE WORK OF THE SPIRIT

Finally, and perhaps in dialectical tension with my last point, this book attends to the way in which the Spirit is *extensively* present in the world in order to create the multiple *intensities* of God's presence in the contingencies of the present created order.[9] Let me unpack what I mean by this thick analysis. As an act of the Holy Spirit, the church is established as a community of the intensive presence of God for passionate, desiring, yearning, active participation in his service and his purposes. The Spirit who is present extensively in the world dwells intensively with particular communities in time for the service and performance of God's will. The church is not, therefore, a place in which one might think of a dividing line from the world. It is, instead, the people in which the presence of God, which in God's omnipresence cannot be spatially limited, dwells in intensity by the power of his Spirit in a community in time which is enabled to proclaim the Lordship of Jesus Christ and actively to participate in God's salvific and redemptive work for all creation. Focusing on the work of the Holy Spirit opens one up to being able to see multiple intensities of God's Spirit throughout the world. And we have been pointed towards this in the call to live in the yearning hope

---

or Pietistic Personalism?: The Problem of the Holy Spirit in Evangelical Theology', in *New Perspectives for Evangelical Theology: Engaging with God, Scripture and the World*, ed. Tom Greggs (Abingdon: Routledge, 2010).

9   Language of 'intensity' and 'extensity' is borrowed from Daniel W. Hardy, *Finding the Church* (London: SCM, 2001). For more on the dynamic operations of the Spirit and the Son in salvation in relation to God's universal and particular works, see Tom Greggs, *Barth, Origen, and Universal Salvation: Restoring Particularity* (Oxford: Oxford University Press, 2009), esp. chapters 5 and 7.

of the transformation of *all things*.

In John's Gospel, in chapter 4, there is a dialogue between Jesus and a member of another religious community – a Samaritan woman. In the course of this conversation, Jesus speaks in terms of the coming hour (from the point of view of the *eschaton*), when true worshipers will worship the Father in Spirit and truth. He asserts that religious propriety is not the issue in terms of who these worshippers will be: worship will not simply be localised to Gerezim (where the Samaritan's temple was – 'this mountain', in the text), or even to Jerusalem (where the Jewish temple was), because worship will involve full reality ('truth') and will be determined by the presence of the Spirit who blows wherever he wills (John 3:8). The Spirit does not make people worship in Jerusalem, even though Jerusalem is the 'correct' place to worship; the precise point is that worship of God cannot be spatio-religiously defined. True worship of the Father is in Spirit and truth; it is not about a 'religious feeling', but about a mode of desire for God. The activity of the Spirit is broader and wider than the confines of the church, and *in different and particularised* ways, the Spirit makes his presence known.

Thinking about the fruits of the Spirit might well be a good way to understand the multiply intensive presence of the Spirit who is extensively and multiply intensively present in the world, and who is the operating condition for true worship of the Father, as the one who is present in all of the reality (and truth) of particular life and who is the foretaste of the coming eschatological community. Where we see individuals and communities displaying the fruits of God's Holy Spirit, we must surely recognise creation flourishing in individuals and communities governed and ruled by the Spirit of our God.

* * *

What has been presented in this chapter has been a reflection of five motifs in pneumatology, arising from the papers and sermons given at The Holy Spirit in the World Today conference. These themes are obviously far from exhaustive, but are presented in the hope of continued reflection on the doctrine of the Spirit as the church continues to move through the twenty-first century. Few features of the church in the world today are more remarkable than the renewed focus on and desire for the Holy Spirit. The purpose of this reflection is, therefore, not merely to engage in repetition of the other chapters, but to offer some themes in anticipation and hopeful expectation of continued engagement in thinking through the doctrine of the Holy Spirit by church people, leaders and academics alike. If theology is to continue to seek to serve the church, then it will need in every place and age to think through and rethink the doctrine of the Holy Spirit anew and afresh.

SPTC Books

Holy Trinity Brompton launched St Paul's Theological Centre in 2005, following the worldwide growth of Alpha and the establishment of HTB as a major resourcing centre for other churches in the UK. SPTC continues to play a key role in the ministry of Alpha International and as developer of theological resources. In addition, in 2007 it became part of St Mellitus College, the newest theological college of the Church of England. St Mellitus is a pioneer in 'church-based' training, preparing students for ordination through a mixture of classroom learning and on the job church ministry. Working through Alpha International and St Mellitus, SPTC has sponsored a number of significant theological conferences, produced the popular GodPod podcast, and begun to plant branches around the world.

The central vision of SPTC is to help 'bring theology back to the heart of the church'. Rather than doing theology in a university or seminary setting, SPTC links its theology and its training as closely as possible to the life of the local church. The Centre is developing a rich seam of theological reflection on church life, following themes that arise from Christian ministry in churches like HTB, and those who use the Alpha course around the world. SPTC Books is an imprint of Alpha International, designed to help develop this theological work. It seeks to publish work linked in one way or another to the wider Alpha network, exploring theology in a way that is truly ecumenical. We will bring together the best of all kinds of theology from all parts of the church – all who are held together by a common belief in the God revealed in Jesus Christ and in the expectation of the presence and power of the Hoy Spirit as the one who makes true worshipful theology possible.

For more information on SPTC, please see:

sptc.htb.org.uk

Or contact:

Alpha International
Holy Trinity Brompton
Brompton Road
London
SW7 1JA

Tel: 0845 644 7544

Email: info@alpha.org

If you would like a copy of the Alpha Publications Brochure,
which includes SPTC's publications, please contact the Alpha
Publications Hotline on:
Tel: 0845 7581 278
To order from overseas:
Tel: +44 1228 611749
Or order online:
alphashop.org